Michael Langford studied Philosophy, Politics and Economics at New College, Oxford, where he was a pupil of H.L.A. Hart, Isaiah Berlin and Stuart Hampshire. Following periods as chaplain to Queens' College, Cambridge and as a Ph.D student in philosophy, he spent 29 years teaching philosophy in Canada. In retirement he teaches, part-time, in the Divinity Faculty at Cambridge. He is married to the sinologist, Dr Sally Church, and they have two daughters. His principal hobbies are Aikido (he is a sandan) and string quartets (in which he plays violin).

Designed for an international readership, *Introduction to Western Moral Philosophy* combines examination of critical thinking with an account of key philosophers in the moral philosophical tradition. These philosophers are not taken as "authorities" to be blindly followed, but as thinkers whose key insights no subsequent philosopher can ignore. The book is based on lectures, given in Canada and Cambridge, at first- year university level.

In three places the book invites the reader to go beyond the introductory stage; first, in a discussion of the proper relationship of philosophy to religion (which has been widely misunderstood); second, in a discussion of the controversial issue of free will; third – following an account of the contemporary failure to find any generally acceptable moral philosophy – Professor Langford outlines his own proposal for such a philosophy.

Cover Image: Frontispiece to *Europe: A Prophecy* by William Blake (1757-1827)
© Fitzwilliam Museum, Cambridge

Usually referred to as *The Ancient of Days*, It shows Blake's embodiment of reason and law creating the universe, with the light coming from his hand representing an architect's compass. Each copy was hand-tinted and is unique; this one is held at the Fitzwilliam Museum of the University of Cambridge.

AN INTRODUCTION TO WESTERN MORAL PHILOSOPHY

Key People and Issues

Michael J. Langford

Emeritus Professor of Philosophy,
Memorial University of Newfoundland, Canada

Faculty of Divinity, University of Cambridge

First published in Great Britain in 2018 by Cambridge Text Education

Copyright @ Michael Langford 2018

The moral right of the author has been asserted

All rights reserved

No part of this publication may be reproduced, stored in a retrieval system, or transmitted, in any form or by any means, without the prior permission in writing of the publisher, nor be otherwise circulated in any form of binding or cover other than that in which it is published and without a similar condition including this condition being imposed on the subsequent purchaser.

A CIP catalogue record for this book is available from the British Library

ISBN 978-1-78971-000-7

Printed and bound in Great Britain by Elitian Ltd, Cambridge

CAMBRIDGE TEXT EDUCATION LTD
www.cambridgetexteducation.com

TABLE OF CONTENTS

Chapter 1. Introduction: What is Western moral philosophy?   1

Chapter 2. The story of Socrates and his claim: "I know that I know nothing"   12

A reading from Plato's Apology

Questions and comments

Chapter 3. Plato and his Dialogues   25

A reading from the Republic

Questions and comments

Chapter 4. Aristotle's virtue ethics   39

Readings from the Nichomachean Ethics

Questions and comments

Chapter 5. Stoics, Epicureans and the emergence of Christian moral philosophy (with special reference to Origen and Augustine)   55

A section on the relation of philosophy to religion

Readings on the "just war"

Questions and comments

Chapter 6. Thomas Aquinas and natural law   79
Readings from the Summa Theologiae
Questions and comments

Chapter 7. Hobbes and the impact of materialism   96
Readings from Hobbes
Questions and comments

Chapter 8. Hume and the Enlightenment   115
Readings from Hume
Questions and comments

Chapter 9. J.S. Mill and Utilitarianism   128
A reading from J.S. Mill's On Liberty
Questions and comments

Chapter 10. Kant and "deontology"   143
A reading from Kant
Questions and comments

Chapter 11. The contemporary scene: Virtue Ethics, Utilitarianism, Kant and Rawls, Emotivism, Moral Realism, Marxist and Neo-Marxist theories, Existentialist theories, Postmodernism, Nihilism   159
Questions and comments

Chapter 12. Some conclusions. The fundamental and abiding questions of moral philosophy   184

TIMELINE

Names and themes referred to in this book.

The letter c stands for the Latin circa, meaning "about". BCE stands for Before the Common Era and CE Common Era (rather than BC and AD).

c. 1000-400 BCE	The "axial" period
c. 600-300 BCE	The high point of classical Greek culture
c. 570-495 BCE	Pythagoras
c. 470-399 BCE	Socrates
c. 428-348 BCE	Plato (founder of the Academy)
c. 384-322 BCE	Aristotle (founder of the Lyceum, or the "Peripatetic" School of Philosophy)
356-323 BCE	Alexander the Great (whose conquests helped to spread Greek ideas across the Mediterranean and the Middle East)
c. 341-270 BCE	Epicurus (founder of the Epicurean School of Philosophy)
c. 336-264 BCE	Zeno of Citium (founder of Stoicism)
c. 287-212 BCE	Archimedes
c. 5 BCE - c. 35 CE	Probable dates for the life of Jesus of Nazareth
c. 185-254 CE	Origen of Alexandria
c. 204-269 CE	Plotinus (the principal figure in Neoplatonism)
c. 312	Conversion of the Emperor Constantine to Christianity, followed by the gradual

	development of "Christendom" in much of Europe, in which church and state became intermingled for centuries
c. 354-430	Augustine (Bishop of Hippo in North Africa)
632	Death of the prophet Muhammad, followed by the rapid spread of Islam
c. 1070 onwards	Revival of learning in the 12th-century
1224-1274	Thomas Aquinas (Christian philosopher and author of the *Summa Theologiae*)
c. 1300-1500	The beginnings of the Renaissance, starting in Italy
1455	The first printed book in Europe (the Gutenberg Bible)
1473-1543	Copernicus
1517	The beginning of the Reformation and the rise of Protestantism
1561-1626	Francis Bacon
1564-1642	Galileo
1583-1645	Hugo Grotius
1596-1650	Rene Descartes
1588-1679	Thomas Hobbes
1632-1677	Baruch Spinoza
1632-1704	John Locke
1643-1727	Isaac Newton
1646-1716	Gottfried Leibniz
1711-1776	David Hume
1724-1804	Immanuel Kant
1748-1832	Jeremy Bentham

1751-1765	The *Encyclopédie*, edited by Diderot in Paris
1770-1831	G.W.F. Hegel
1806-1883	John Stuart Mill
1818-1883	Karl Marx
1844-1900	Friedrich Nietzsche
1873-1958	G.E. Moore
1889-1951	Ludwig Wittgenstein
1898-1979	Herbert Marcuse
1905-1980	Jean-Paul Sartre
1907-1992	H.L.A. Hart
1908-1979	Charles L. Stevenson
1910-1989	A.J. Ayer
1919-2002	Richard Hare
1920-2010	Philippa Foot
1921-2002	John Rawls
1922 (born)	John Searle
1924-1998	Jean-Francois Lyotard
1926-1984	Michel Foucault
1944 (born)	Simon Blackburn

GLOSSARY

Agape, Eros, Philia – 3 key terms denoting love in Greek. *Agape* was rarely used in Classical Greek until the first century CE and referred to an unconditional love or regard for God or for fellow humans. It will be discussed in Chapter 12. *Eros*, in more recent writings, has tended to denote sexual love, but in Plato it was a much broader term (although it could include sexual desire) and was associated with an intense desire for beauty. *Philia* refers to friendship and loyalty. According to Aristotle, in its highest form it is a virtue impelling one to value the other person alongside oneself.

Allegory – a work of art such as a story or painting in which the characters, narrative, etc. represent something else; in other words, a complex form of metaphor.

Atheism – the denial that there are gods or a God.

Bible – the sacred book of the Christians, containing the *Old Testament* (which is also sacred to Judaism, and was originally written in Hebrew) and the *New Testament*, originally written in Greek. The *Old Testament* dates to the first millennium BCE, while most of the *New Testament* dates probably to 50-90 CE.

Catholic – when written with the lower case "c", this is usually an adjective that refers to more conservative forms of Christianity; when written with the upper case (C), it is short for Roman Catholic.

Classical Utilitarianism – this philosophy is defined in terms of the view that what is morally good should be seen as the course of action that will provide the greatest happiness for the greatest number, in the long term. Utilitarianism, without the qualification "classical", is a much vaguer term, suggesting that the consequences of our actions for some kind of usefulness are the primary ground for moral evaluation.

Deontology – a moral philosophy that defines what is good in terms of abiding by moral principles or duties. *Deontos* is the Greek word for "duty".

Dialectic – a Greek word that means discussion or debate, but which acquired a technical sense in Plato, meaning an organized dialogue in which truth emerges.

Dialogue – a conversation between two or more participants. The term is also used to refer to the written works of Plato, which were nearly all in dialogue form.

Empiricism – a reference to what can be learned through systematic observation or experimentation using our five senses. In chapter 10 we shall see how the philosophical term *a posteriori* has a very similar meaning.

Essence – the term, derived from Greek philosophy, for what is claimed to be the real nature of things, especially human beings. Whether or not human beings have "essences" in this sense is one of the issues raised by existentialists.

Existence – in existentialist writings this term does not simply refer to the mere fact of being alive in the world, but to the actual, lived experience of what it is like to have the kind of inner world that we discover.

Homosexuality – literally, in mixed Greek and Latin, "same sex", which can refer either to an attraction to members of the same gender or to sexual activity with members of the same gender.

Idealism – a philosophical theory in which ideas such as "love" or "table" constitute what is ultimately real, rather than individual objects.

Irony – the use of either a situation or a form of words through which (often by use of a kind of contradiction or paradox), a subtle truth emerges.

Ineffability – The view that God, or ultimate reality, is beyond any rational account. Denials of total ineffability do not claim that God or ultimate reality can be fully or adequately understood, but that, perhaps through metaphor and analogy, some glimmerings of genuine understanding are possible.

Metaphor – a figure of speech in which words are stretched to give different meanings. Sometimes there is a clear contrast between a literal sense and a metaphorical sense; for example, if we speak of a "dark" day, the literal sense of "dark" would imply a day in which there was little sunlight, but the metaphorical sense would imply a day in which there was sadness. Natural language, literature and poetry rely heavily on the use of metaphor. Sometimes the word "metaphorical" is also applied to situations as well as to words or phrases, and then the term has some similarities with the notion of "irony".

An illustration of when metaphor can refer to a situation rather than to a word or phrase may help. In a poem called *Inchcape Rock*, by Robert Southey (1802), an ancient story is retold in which a pirate captain removes a bell that had been attached to a dangerous reef. Some time later, because the warning bell was no longer there, the pirate himself is wrecked on this same reef during a storm. The situation can be seen as a metaphor for the way in which evil deeds end up hurting the evildoer. We may recall Plato's argument that failing to respond to the good damages your soul. The bell story is, at the same time, deeply ironic.

Metaphysics – literally "after the Physics" (see chapter 1, note 7). Because of Aristotle's discussion of what he considered to be ultimate reality in his book with this name, the term has been used to refer to any subsequent discussion of fundamental issues relating to reality.

Monism – from the Greek word for "one", refers to a philosophical or religious theory in which the fundamental unity, or oneness, of all things is stressed.

Myth – a story (usually ancient, and often involving divine beings) in which some kind of psychological or moral truth is conveyed indirectly. It can also legitimate or justify an ideology, practice or social system.

Ontology – from the Greek *ontos*, meaning being or reality; the inquiry into what is believed to be the underlying or basic ground of all that exists.

Oracle – a place or a person, where it was believed that the words of a god could be found, especially words that could answer questions put to the oracle. Delphi is the most famous Greek example.

Oratory – the effective use of speech, especially in public debate.

Original Sin – a Christian doctrine that exists in many forms and teaches that all humans are characterized by a sinful nature. In Catholic and early Protestant teaching it is held to be "genetic" — acquired through our descent from Adam and Eve. In the Greek Orthodox tradition (and in liberal Protestantism) it refers not to an original guilt, but to a universal moral weakness. Its relevance for moral philosophy will emerge in chapter 6 and in the discussion of Marxism.

Orthodox – when written with the lower case (o) this refers to more traditional views, in many contexts; when written with an upper case (O) it refers to the Eastern Orthodox churches that have never accepted the overall spiritual leadership of the Bishop of Rome (the Pope).

Pantheism – the theory that the cosmos can be identified with the divine. Panentheism argues that while God is embodied in the universe, there is also an aspect of God that is apart and beyond it.

Parable – as with an allegory, a story that is not meant to be taken literally but made up in order to illustrate a moral or spiritual truth; whereas a myth tends to grow within a culture, rather than being a deliberate invention.

Passion – in modern English, "passion" tends to refer to very strong or overriding emotions. For Hume, it was a more general term for the emotional side of human nature.

Phenomenology – a set of approaches that analyses human experience from the standpoint of human consciousness, rather than in terms of "external", empirical evidence.

Predestination – the doctrine that individuals are destined to achieve salvation before they are born. The term covers a variety of theories, including those arguing that some individuals are predestined for damnation. All appear to be in tension with the ultimate reality of free will.

Protestant – a general term for the churches whose origins arise in the Reformation, spearheaded by Luther in 1517.

Reductionism – simplification of phenomena to the smallest number of constituent parts. One example might be the description of a wide variety of "abnormal" behaviours seen in many individuals as manifestations of a single psychological disorder or syndrome.

Religion – a very hard word to define, sometimes thought to derive from a Latin word meaning to "bind", though this is disputed. The relationship to philosophy is discussed in chapter 5.

Rhetoric – the art of using words to persuade others, typically in either a court of law or a political assembly.

Secularism – the word "secular" is often contrasted with sacred. It means what is ordinary or everyday, whereas sacred means what is "set apart". The term secularism is derived from "secular" and was coined in the 19th century. It has two rather different senses. It can mean a philosophical approach that is independent of any religious point of view, or it can mean a philosophical approach that is positively antagonistic to any religious point of view. The former, more positive account (within a philosophy of secular humanism), can be found in the writings of Corliss Lamont (his *Philosophy of Humanism* is online at https://www.corliss-lamont.org/philos8.pdf). The latter, more negative account, can be found in the writings of Richard Norman (e.g. *On Humanism*. London: Routledge, 2012).

Semantics – an inquiry into the meaning of words or expressions.

Sophistry – the clever use of words in order to persuade others, regardless of the truth.

Theism – from the Greek word for a god or God (*theos*); now used, primarily, to refer to belief in a single and personal God, responsible for creating the cosmos and continually intervening in it. "Personal" means having relationships with individual human beings. However, in ancient Greece, *theos* was used much more loosely, for any belief in gods or God.

Theology – the academic study of religions, especially those that have concepts of God (Greek *theos*).

Utility – for Hume, this was a general term for what is useful for human life. Only later, with writers such as J.S. Mill, did it develop the more technical sense of "what will promote the greatest happiness of the greatest number".

Chapter 1. Introduction: What is Western moral philosophy?

1. What is *philosophy*?

The word *philosophy* means literally the "the love of wisdom". It comes from two Greek words: *philia*, which is one of the Greek words for love (it is often used to mean friendship); and *sophia*, which is usually translated as "wisdom". However, the literal translation does not really help us to understand what Western philosophy actually is until we see how the term has been *used* within a tradition going back to the Greek world of around 600 to 300 BCE. This tradition of philosophy has two characteristics and the main purpose of this introductory chapter is to explain these. First, it refers to a method of critical thinking and second, it emphasizes a body of fundamental or seminal texts, many of which students of philosophy are expected to be familiar with. Let us look at these two characteristics. In the next chapter we shall see how the first characteristic relates to the historical life and teachings of Socrates, and in subsequent chapters how it relates to a series of other Western philosophers who have been of major influence.

2. A method of critical thinking

In critical thinking we find a sharp contrast between reason and authority as sources of knowledge. Aware of how different cultures and different authority figures often teach contradictory things, many of the Greek thinkers who were called philosophers attempted to find *reasons* for their beliefs, in contrast with the acceptance of beliefs on the basis of authority. Plato put the matter like this in the *Theaetetus*: genuine knowledge, which the Greeks called *episteme*, has not only to be true, or correct. We also need a good reason for holding it, ideally by providing a *proof*[1] to show that it is true. Believing something only because we have been told it, on authority, is not enough. Even if what we believe happens to be true, this is more a matter of luck than of reasoning, and Plato said that in such cases we had true opinion rather than knowledge. Moreover, when people rely solely on authority, they often believe contradictory, and sometimes ridiculous, things[2]. *Knowledge* has to be founded on reason and evidence and argument.

During the course of this book the nature of critical thinking should become clearer, starting with Socrates' search for true knowledge rather than opinion based on authority. Among the characteristics that emerge will be: (i) seeking to avoid contradictions or paradoxes whenever possible; (ii) searching for the kind of evidence that is appropriate for holding a position; (iii) clarifying the meaning of terms that are used; (iv) listening to the other side of an argument. This topic will be revisited in the discussion of rationality in the last chapter.

---

[1] Plato used the Greek word *logos*, which can mean "reason", or "proof", or – in some contexts, "word".

[2] Socrates did not mean that there is no place for any authority – for example, when we learn a foreign language we ask experts the meaning of words – but this is quite different from accepting fundamental truths on mere authority, concerning, for example, religion or politics, about which there is serious and legitimate disagreement. It must also be remembered that Plato, in his *Republic*, did not simply lay down his system, he also produced a sustained *argument* for it. Even if we agree that his argument is sometimes flawed, this distances his approach from a pure authoritarianism. Subsequently, Plato made substantial changes to his political ideas, favouring a rigid system of laws rather than rule by a rigorously educated elite.

3. A body of fundamental texts

The collection of fundamental writings that philosophers use keeps growing, and there will always be controversy concerning what should be included. Today, it certainly includes the Dialogues of Plato and we shall understand why this is so during the third chapter. New texts keep being added; for example, some of the writings of Wittgenstein in the 20th century. Interestingly, there can arise a tension between the first characteristic (a method of critical thinking) and this second characteristic (a body of fundamental texts), because as soon as any of these texts becomes a kind of authority, then the spirit of critical thinking is threatened. This actually happens in certain schools of philosophy, in which some writings are so powerful that they become just the kind of authority that critical thinking was meant to liberate us from. In view of this danger, I suggest that the best way to see this body of writings is as examples of critical thinking. They are also attempts to answer the central questions that philosophy raises, examples against which we can "bounce off" our own ideas. We take the texts seriously, not because we are always expected to agree with the arguments or the answers suggested, but because they help us to be aware of the many different arguments and answers that have been given. This can help us to clarify and inform our own thinking. When it comes to the more obvious arguments, we don't have to keep "reinventing the wheel". As I have indicated, these texts, directly or indirectly, all concern the traditional and fundamental questions that have been raised within Western philosophy, such as "What is knowledge?"

This body of literature has another function, namely to facilitate a set of metaphors and expressions that become a kind of common currency, thereby making communication richer. Outside the domain of philosophy, all those educated in ancient Greece shared the poems of Homer – thus providing a rich source of language, expression and metaphor. Similarly, most educated people in Britain have some familiarity with an equivalent body of shared literature (such as the *King James Version* of the Bible[3] and the works of Shakespeare), again enabling the use of myriad metaphors and expressions (like "the tower of Babel", "this mortal coil", and "a plague on both your houses")[4]. Similarly again, most educated Chinese have some familiarity with great Tang poets, such as Du Fu, with the same result. In the case of Western philosophy, these analogies can help to explain one aspect of the usefulness of a widely-consulted body of texts. Even in this book a number of the expressions and metaphors that recur will be found. Examples include, Plato's cave, Descartes' dualism, the state of nature, the rights of man, the naturalistic fallacy – all of which can both provide lively images and act as a kind of shorthand for describing quite complex ideas. Again, the point is not that an authoritative truth is being laid down, but that insight and communication are enhanced.

4. Western and Eastern philosophy

These two criteria for Western philosophy can help us to see why some people want to contrast it with Eastern philosophy. Here we have to be very careful. In my view, much of what Westerners refer to as Eastern philosophy can be just as critical and open-minded as Western philosophy. However, it is also true that there is a danger

---

[3] The translation of the Hebrew and Greek scriptures into English, at the command of James I of England, finished in 1611.

[4] The importance of these shared metaphors and expressions explains why it is so important for educational policy to stress a body of traditional literature (or a "canon") that most schoolchildren will gain some familiarity with. The downside may be an undue conservatism, but without a familiarity with this canon children risk cultural impoverishment.

Introduction: What is Western moral philosophy?

– as in the West – of taking philosophy to be the teaching of a *school* of thought. So, for example, a course teaching the Confucian classics might treat these classics as especially authoritative, not only in the sense of representing what Confucianism is, but also in representing the *correct* approach to philosophical issues.

An additional caution concerns any sharp division of philosophy into Western and Eastern. Particularly since the 17th century (when, for example, the German philosopher Leibniz began to study the Chinese classics), there has been a growing international dialogue on philosophical issues. Further, many important philosophers, for example in the Islamic world, do not fit neatly into a Western/Eastern divide.

Despite my reservations concerning a division into Western and Eastern philosophy, the writers who feature in this book, starting with some of the Greeks, are all clearly Western, and were thinking and writing in the context of a tradition that began shortly before the time of Socrates. This explains the title and emphases of this book. Nevertheless, there will be occasional references to Chinese and other Eastern philosophers, such as Mozi.

5. Philosophy and moral philosophy or ethics

This book concerns *moral* philosophy, which is one branch of philosophy. However, there is often an overlap with other branches — for example, metaphysics (the study of what is claimed to be ultimate reality) and the philosophy of biology (for example, when the question is raised concerning whether or not we can be said to have *free will*). Sometimes moral philosophy is called *ethics*, and the reason for this is that the basic use of the words "morality" and "ethics" is almost identical. "Morality" comes from the Latin word *mores*, while "ethics" comes from the equivalent Greek word, *ethos*.

Both terms, in their original settings, could mean "custom". It is easy to see that in any culture, some customs are not treated simply as how things are *usually* done, but how things ought to be done. Usually, telling the truth, especially to friends and family, is not only something that is *generally* done, it is something that nearly all of us feel *ought* to be done. In other words, over time, some customs become treated as so important that they need to be encouraged or even enforced. A penalty for non-observance, a penalty that philosophers call a sanction, comes into effect, either by coercive, legal force, or by a kind of social pressure, such as verbal criticism. Here we can see how a distinction can be made between *legal* and *moral* rules, despite many examples of overlap. The typical sanction for legal rules is coercive, as when those convicted of a legal offence are put in prison; while the typical sanction for moral rules is a different kind of pressure, such as public criticism. Refraining from robbery is *both* a legal and a moral rule; being nice to our grandmothers is a moral rule but not a legal rule. Returning our tax forms on a particular day is a legal rule but – arguably at least – not a moral rule.[5]

A consequence of this origin of the words is that in English the words "morality" and "ethics" are very similar, although practice has led to some differences of emphasis.[6] In this book I shall not make

---

[5] There is an interesting complication here. Many people ague that – at least within a democratic regime – we have a general *moral* obligation to obey the law, so that filling in our tax returns by the day demanded by law is a *moral* obligation as well as a legal one. The strictly legal rules are often called civil law (from the Roman *ius civile*), in contrast with moral law. A clearer example of a distinction between legal and moral obligation is evident in outrageous political regimes, like that of Nazi Germany, where the civil law of that regime – such as one that demanded the persecution of Jews – was sometimes in contravention of moral law.

[6] On this matter see Bernard Williams, *Ethics and the Limits of Philosophy* (Cambridge, Mass. Harvard University Press, 1985), p. 6.

any distinction between the terms.

6. Greek philosophy as a starting point

As many historians have reminded us, there was a kind of intellectual explosion starting around 1000 BCE, not only in Greece, but in many other parts of the world: the Hebrew prophets, like Isaiah and Jeremiah; the *Upanishads* and early Buddhism in India; Zoroaster/Zarathustra in Iran (although his dates may be earlier); and the "sages" (*shengren*) of China. This intellectual explosion has led some historians to refer to the time as the "Axial Age".

The Greek culture of the classical period, roughly from 600 to 300 BCE, was extraordinary in a number of ways. In the arts, naturalistic works flourished in both painting and sculpture. The theatre became a popular medium for both entertainment and intellectual challenge. In economics, we find an increased use of coinage (invented in Turkey in the seventh century BCE) which enormously facilitated international trade. In politics, we find the first experiments in what would become democracies, in which ordinary citizens, often selected by ballot, helped govern their country. In mathematics and engineering (the latter, notably, in the work of Archimedes), the Greeks made huge strides. Also, during this period, we find the first sustained attempt at critical thinking.

I am not claiming a total originality for Greek culture in any of these areas. The contributions of earlier thinkers and artists in other parts of the world to Greek culture is still debated and some of its early philosophers were subjects of the Persian Empire. Also, we have to admit to ignorance of many ancient cultures where there may have been individuals who were forerunners in all these areas. Nevertheless, the contribution of classical Greek culture to our world is extraordinary, and it has a particular importance for the theme of this book. There are, therefore, good grounds for beginning a survey of Western moral philosophy by exploring some of the greatest philosophers in ancient Greece.

7. Meta-ethics and practical ethics

Many philosophers distinguish two kinds of moral philosophy. One, called *meta-ethics*, is the study of questions such as: "How do we know what is right and wrong?" and "Does what is right and wrong depend on religion, or is it independent of religion?"[7] The other is often called *practical ethics* and refers to the inquiry into specific questions or issues such as: "Is it right for a state to use capital punishment?" and "Is it ever right for a private citizen to refuse to fight in a war?" When we hear that there has been a discussion of a moral or ethical issue, perhaps at a private occasion such as a dinner party, usually what this means is that a practical issue has been discussed, and – very probably – that there has been some disagreement.

Does it follow that these discussions have been philosophical? Not necessarily. If those taking part in a debate have simply expressed their opinions, then this was not a philosophical debate. However, if they seriously argued their case, offering reasons for their opinions, then the debate was probably, at least in part, philosophical and would be an example of practical ethics. If the reasons offered

---

[7] The word "meta" comes from a Greek word that means "after". One of Aristotle's books was called the *Metaphysics* simply because in editions of his works it was usually placed *after* the book he called the *Physics*. The *Metaphysics* deals with Aristotle's concerns with what we might term ultimate reality, including questions concerning the reality and nature of God. As a result – since the time of Aristotle – the term has been taken to refer to *foundational* questions, such as those that inquire about the nature of the universe. Thus, in the history of philosophy, *meta-ethics* has been coined – as a kind of parallel to metaphysics – to refer to fundamental questions concerning the nature of ethics.

Introduction: What is Western moral philosophy?

were linked to a theory of what made these reasons relevant, then we almost certainly had what I would call a philosophical debate in a deeper sense, and some meta-ethical issues would have been raised.

It follows that it is not always easy to make a sharp distinction between the two branches of ethics, because as soon as *reasons* start to be offered for a particular point of view on a practical issue, then there is likely to be at least an implicit appeal to some theory of what makes actions or people good or bad. For example, later in this book we shall examine the theory known as *utilitarianism*, according to which actions are good or bad depending on how far they promote or fail to promote general happiness. It is usually described, in what is often called "classical utilitarianism", by the phrase, "the greatest happiness of the greatest number" – a term that will be examined in chapter 9. It follows that when the argument depends on pointing to the alleged consequences of an action, then an appeal to meta-ethics may be involved.

Some writers make a distinction between moral philosophy and political philosophy, the former relating to more personal issues in human relationships, the latter to more communal issues concerning the kind of social or political order that we should promote. But many philosophers treat political philosophy as a branch of moral philosophy, and this is the approach generally taken in this book. Thus, "Is it right for a state to use capital punishment?" is approached as an issue in practical ethics.

Some, like Aristotle, see the matter the other way round. Aristotle centred his ethics on the issue of what would make a good citizen. In the area of political philosophy there is an analogous distinction between "meta" questions, such as: "Should all states develop into liberal democracies?"; and more "practical" issues, such as: "At what age should citizens be allowed to vote?"

This book is primarily a book of meta-ethics. It examines the history of ethical thinking and uses critical thinking to assess many of the great theories that have been brought forward. It also examines the more general questions about the good life that have been asked. However, as indicated, it is often hard to disentangle the two aspects of ethics in actual debate, and practical issues will quite often be raised in the main body of the text, and frequently in the questions that follow at the end of the chapters.

The book is written roughly at the level of a first year undergraduate course (which I have taught both in Canada and in Cambridge), and should be accessible to the ordinary reader who is interested in philosophical issues. I have in mind an international audience, which is why I often add background notes that may be helpful to readers who are less familiar with Western history, and glossaries, for those whose first language in not English, or who have not come across some of the terms that are commonly used in philosophical argument.

8. The structure of this book

The following chapters include extended quotations and topics for consideration. Following these suggested questions, for private thought or group discussion, I shall indicate some of the answers that might be given, and how all of them – in turn – invite further questions. In this way it should become evident how both philosophy in general – and moral philosophy in particular – is an *ongoing* tradition. Progress of a kind may be made in that some deeper understanding of the issues can be realized and the significance of new questions can be appreciated. Nevertheless, philosophy is a

Introduction: What is Western moral philosophy?

kind of adventure that can go on forever. As in science, every time a question seems to be answered, more questions emerge.[8] If Socrates was right to claim that "the unexamined life is not worth living", at least part of what he meant is that pursuing the great questions asked by philosophers (even if we do not achieve clear and definite answers) is natural to the human spirit. It is at least part of what a rich and fulfilled human life is all about. Sometimes the active pursuit of this adventure has practical implications (for example, about how we should educate our children or organize our societies), but even when it does not, it may have a kind of intrinsic value – akin to the value of experiencing great music or of pursuing scientific knowledge for its own sake.

---

[8] The English word "science" comes from the Latin *scientia*, which – in turn – can be a translation of *episteme* (the Greek word for "true knowledge"). Originally, *episteme* was thought to refer to any genuine body of knowledge, but for many Greeks the paradigm example was geometry because here the truths discovered (for example, in Pythagoras' theorem) were seen to be eternal, and independent of space and time. It was only after around 1500 that *empirical* truths (discovered in a scientific method that included observation and experiment in time) came to be seen as paradigm examples of what people referred to as "science". In the 21st century intellectual disciplines tend to be divided into four categories, although these are not watertight: (i) mathematics (where the truths discovered do not depend on observation in the real world); (ii) the "hard sciences", notably physics, chemistry, biology and geology (where the empirical method is paramount); (iii) the social sciences, such as sociology and archaeology (where empirical data and theory are intermingled); (iv) the humanities, such as literature, history, musicology and theology (where empirical data, although sometimes relevant, is secondary to theory). There is often strong disagreement as to exactly how to classify some intellectual disciplines, such as psychology, history or linguistics. (For example, the Italian philosopher Giambattista Vico [1668-1744] thought that history was the paramount example of science.) Philosophy is usually classed as one of the humanities, but – in my view – one of the questions that philosophers should be asking is whether this fourfold division can stand up to critical examination.

Chapter 2. The story of Socrates and his claim: "I know that I know nothing"

Background

During the classical period of Greek history (c. 600-300 BCE), there was no unified state for the whole region, but hundreds of city-states, each of which was called a *polis*. This is the Greek word that is the origin of the English word "politics". Most were within the region that is now the nation of Greece, including a large number of islands, but some were in what is now part of Turkey. Each city-state consisted of a central city and a surrounding area of countryside, where there were usually farms. The smallest ones may have had populations of only a few thousand (comprising male citizens, women, children, resident aliens and slaves); the largest, including Athens, had populations of over 200,000. Some were ruled by tyrants, or a group of aristocrats. Others, including Athens, were democracies, at least for much of their histories, in which all male citizens held power through assemblies and juries. The city-states were frequently at war with each other (with all citizens expected to serve time in the army), but many of them also co-operated, forming alliances in order to face more powerful city-states or external enemies, such as the Persian Empire. They shared a common language and culture, including a poetic tradition rooted in Homer (c. 700 BCE).

The story of Socrates and his claim

1. Socrates

Socrates was born in Athens around 470 BCE. He was a citizen, neither rich nor poor, and possibly a sculptor by trade, as – it has been claimed – was his father. He was married and had children, though it was said that he and his wife had a somewhat tense relationship. Like most citizens he served in the citizen army, where he appears to have shown considerable courage during his military service. Early in life he was attracted to the tradition of Greek philosophy, especially the group discussion of fundamental issues, and – like many other philosophers – he gathered a group of young men around him. They sat at his feet, listening to him and sometimes joining in the discussions. The Greek word for discussion or debate was *dialectic* and for Socrates this term soon acquired a technical sense in which it was sharply distinguished from *rhetoric*, which was "the art of persuasion". Dialectic, Socrates claimed, when properly undertaken, was designed to find out the truth. Rhetoric, which for him held a pejorative[1] sense, was designed to *win* a debate, say in a court of law, regardless of the truth. This distinction led Socrates to attack a group of philosophy teachers called *Sophists*, who – usually for money – trained young men to be orators or lawyers. The English word "sophistry" derives from this term, and means something like "the clever use of words to disguise what is really true". In fact, this is a bit unfair to the Sophists, because, when properly used, there is a place for learning the art of persuasion, or "oratory".

The issue here is very much alive in our day. The advertising industry is designed to persuade rather than to tell scientific truths – although the law usually forbids the telling of outright lies. Similarly,

---

[1] From the Latin, *peior*, meaning "worse".

those trained to prosecute or defend in courts of law, and – in the Western world – those aspiring to represent political parties, are much more likely to be interested in *winning or persuading* than in searching for truth. Sometimes the truth sits uncomfortably with one's case! At the same time, most of us would agree that both rhetoric and oratory have their place, and the problem is not so much their existence as their misuse.[2]

To return to the story of Socrates. Despite the originality of his ideas and the offence he caused to those he criticized, for most of his life his behaviour was tolerated. In fact, the Greek culture of the time was extraordinarily tolerant compared with most cultures, both then and later. Many philosophers not only criticized the conventional religions of the time (still a dangerous activity in many parts of the world), they also made fun of powerful politicians. However, shortly before Socrates' trial, in 399 BCE, things changed. The reason was a political crisis largely caused by defeat in war. As often in such historical situations there was a crackdown on all forms of dissent. The situation in the U.S. during the Cold War comes to mind, when a series of intolerant measures associated with McCarthyism[3]

---

[2] The fact that Socrates was so often in the company of young men has led many to refer to him, and his chief disciple, Plato (who also held discussions with groups of students, or disciples), as homosexual. Girls and young women, in the culture of the time, were not allowed to join in these public discussions – although the evidence suggests that despite this unfairness, a few women did achieve a status as philosophers in the ancient world. The evidence strongly suggests that both Socrates and Plato had romantic attachments to good-looking young men (which did not mean that they could not be married or have girlfriends as well), so that it may well be that in terms of orientation they were – at least in part – homosexual. However, the evidence also suggests (especially in Plato's dialogue called the *Symposium*) that they were opposed to actual sexual intimacy with members of the same sex.

[3] So named after U.S. Senator Joseph McCarthy who had a phobia concerning anything to do with communism.

The story of Socrates and his claim

took hold of the country, brought about by an irrational fear of communism. In particular, some Athenian generals who had lost a battle through no fault of their own were put on trial. Socrates came to their defence; this, in turn, encouraged the prosecutors to go after Socrates, accusing him of (i) atheism and (ii) corrupting Athenian youth.

The truth of the matter was as follows: with regards to atheism, Socrates had made fun of the stories of the Greek gods – who, according to popular legends lived on Mount Olympus and lived lives full of sex and violence. Like many other educated Athenians, Socrates thought these stories silly and untrue – though this did not mean that he did not believe in spiritual entities of a kind, who could be called gods. In fact, he also believed in some kind of supernatural influence in his life – one that he referred to as a kind of sign that he received. We shall return to the relationship of philosophy to religion in later chapters. In short, Socrates was certainly not an atheist, but he did attack the popular image of the gods. With regards to the charge of corruption, once again there is a kind of half-truth in the prosecutors' accusation – it depends on what one means by corruption. That he encouraged the young to think for themselves and attack authority, when it was not justified, is certainly true. If a ruler regarded this as corruption – because it might lead to the questioning of his authority – then once again we can understand the charge.

The trial of Socrates was a very public affair, carried out, according to custom, before a large jury made up of fellow citizens. Two of Socrates' followers, Plato and Xenophon, were there, and published details of the trial shortly afterwards, so that we can be pretty sure, at least in general terms, of what happened. Both accounts have survived and Plato's *Apology* (the Greek word for "defence") supplies the text that is included in this chapter.

Central to Socrates' defence is the story he told of how he believed he had a divine mission to educate the young. His story went like this: a close friend (Chaerephon) asked the oracle at Delphi whether there was anyone wiser than Socrates, and received the answer "No".

Here, some explanation is needed. Many ancient cultures had *oracles* where people would regularly go to ask questions of the gods. We might wish to regard these with complete scepticism, thinking that they were simply ways for the oracle's priests to make money, but one can argue for a more complex interpretation. This might stress (i) the psychological need for people to have sources of authority that were separate from the ruling class; (ii) the possibility that some people have a genuine insight or psychic ability, and therefore that, sometimes, helpful answers might be given; and (iii) the possibility that a group of intelligent priests, interpreting the perhaps mumbled words of the oracle (in the case of Delphi, a woman, known as the Pythia, who might well have been under the influence of drugs), actually constructed sensible answers. Part of the motive for such answers might have been financial, but this might not be the whole story. The priests might have been aware of a social responsibility to give sensible advice to all kinds of people.

Puzzled by the reply of the oracle, Socrates began a quest to find a truly wise person – someone who was wiser than he. He went first to the politicians of his day, who certainly thought they were wise, and after questioning them he soon concluded that they were what we might call "windbags" – puffed up with what they thought to be wisdom, but actually empty of real knowledge. Needless to say, this activity, with its exposure of pomposity, tended to make him enemies among the powerful. Next, he went to the poets, and, after debating

The story of Socrates and his claim

with them, he concluded that their poetry often did express profound insight, or wisdom, but that they were unable to *explain* this wisdom in ordinary words. Thus they did not have the kind of knowledge (*episteme* again) that he was looking for. They were *inspired* rather than *wise*. Next he went to the artisans, the skilled workers in (for example) silver and bronze and wood. Here he found great technical know-how, but once again, little knowledge of why the techniques worked. In our own day we might make a similar contrast between the skill of a metalworker and the science (again, *episteme*) of a metallurgist.

Socrates' conclusion was both profound and paradoxical. He concluded his quest by deciding that in a strange way he was, after all, the wisest man in Greece. All these others thought they had wisdom, when in fact they did not, but he at least knew that he had no wisdom. In effect he was saying: "At least I know this – that I know nothing."

Of course, to say "I know nothing" is paradoxical, because to claim that you know nothing, is, in a way, to claim that you do know *something* – namely, that you know nothing! In later philosophy, this kind of situation has led to a host of speculations concerning how to interpret statements that refer, in whole or part, to themselves. These discussions come under the general heading of *the self-referential paradox*, but I shall not address the issues here.

Clearly, in this story, Socrates is being ironic,[4] or perhaps just humorous. He is using a subtle joke to make a serious point, namely

---

[4] Note the contrast, in English, between sarcasm and irony. Sarcasm is a kind of taunting, in which the statements made are obviously false, whereas irony – either by the use of language or action or situation – reveals a kind of deeper or hidden truth that is the opposite of what seems to be the case. Much poetry and literature depend on the subtle use of irony, either by word or action or situation.

that we have to be sceptical; we need to challenge claims to wisdom – like that of the politicians of his day – and more generally, as we have seen, that we have to seek for knowledge rather than opinion. What we have been told is not necessarily true.

To return to the trial: Socrates' vigorous but unconventional defence of his activities convinced some, but not a majority of the jury, who found him guilty. Then – in accordance with the customs of the time – both the prosecutor and the defendant (Socrates) had to suggest a suitable penalty. The prosecutor suggested death. Socrates, instead of a modest fine, suggested that in view of the good he had done to the city by properly educating the youth he should be given a state pension. In the circumstances most of the jury would almost certainly have accepted a modest fine because they did not want an extreme penalty for his crime. However, his act of outrageous defiance so angered the majority that they commanded the death penalty – which was exacted a few days later.

The tolerance of Athens, at the time, is indicated once again by the manner of the death sentence. This was not death by torture or public humiliation, but by the drinking of a poison (hemlock) that would gradually lead to paralysis and death. (Scholars are divided on the issue of how painful the death would have been, given the kind of hemlock that he drank.) Socrates' death and dying words are powerfully portrayed in Plato's dialogue, the *Phaedo*.

Lying, as it were, behind this story of Socrates' trial, there is a huge question that is raised for us – at least indirectly. Socrates felt that he had a mission, a kind of divine mission, because – as he famously put the matter during his defence – "the unexamined life is not worth living". He describes his mission as being like that of a fly that bites a lazy horse in order to goad it into action. Similarly, his mission, he thinks, either by painful questions or by rigorous debate,

The story of Socrates and his claim

is to *awaken* us, so that we can begin to ask ourselves what life is really about. Perhaps there is an element of elitism here. We have to be careful not to denigrate the value of ordinary labour, such as that of the artisans whose skills were admired by Socrates. However, he felt that there was a higher level of being, or living, of which human beings were capable. This was the life of the mind, a life that asked questions, that was genuinely curious about all things and sought for some kind of reason behind the unpredictability of daily life.

Here there is an interesting link between Socrates and earlier philosophers, known as the Pre-Socratics. The first of them was Thales, who taught that "all is water". Apart from the fact that water does seem to be a constituent of all life, the search for an *All* was typical of a Greek search for a unifying principle or principles that would somehow begin to make sense of the manifold complexity of human experience. Understanding what everything was made out of could be seen as a step towards trying to make sense of life, taken as a whole. It was an important step to what would later become science.

In our day, the fundamental question that Socrates was raising was not unlike one of us asking: "What is the meaning of life?" Of course, the answer to this might be: "There is no 'meaning' to life and this is a question that we should not bother either to ask or to answer". In chapter 11 we shall see why a number of 20th century philosophers would respond in this way, but if we are to be sympathetic to classical culture, we have to see that this would not be a natural response for the Greeks. We should at least explore the kinds of answers they might give. Is human life, especially the kind of good life that we should seek for ourselves and for our children, a matter of (a) gaining honour, or (b) happiness, or (c) status, or (d) virtue, or some mixture of these things, or none of the above? Whether or not we think that there is some kind of divine or cosmic "purpose" for the very existence and nature of the universe, this personal question is almost bound to strike every reflective person. "What should be my aim in life?" Even if there is no *extrinsic purpose* for human life, we can choose to give it some kind of purpose, something that will make the human experience more challenging and more worthwhile.

In this context we can begin to see the significance of Socrates' claim: "the unexamined life is not worth living". Not to ask fundamental questions, or not to ponder the great mysteries of life and existence, or not to be full of curiosity and wonder, is not to live a truly human life; it is to live on the level of animals. Similarly, Aristotle taught that philosophy began with a kind of "wonder" (*thaumazein*). Here, once again, we can see that there is a certain kind of elitism in the Greek view of the world, but this does not mean that we should reject it without thought. Socrates' question invites us to consider what kind of life we should be leading, and what kind of life we hope to make available for our children. Is it the case that the thoughtful ("examined") considerations of the scientist, the historian, the philosopher, etc. are in fact what makes life truly worthwhile?

A reading from Plato's *Apology*[5]

I will refer you to a witness who is worthy of credit; that witness shall be the god of Delphi – he will tell you about my wisdom, if I have any, and of what sort it is. You must have known Chaerephon: he was early a friend of mine, and also a friend of yours, for he shared in the recent exile of the people, and returned with you. Well, Chaerephon, as you know, was very impetuous in all his doings, and he went to Delphi and boldly asked the oracle to tell him whether – as I was saying, I must beg you not to interrupt – he asked the oracle to tell him whether anyone was wiser than I was, and the Pythian prophetess answered, that there was no man wiser. Chaerephon is dead himself: but his brother, who is in court, will confirm the truth of what I am saying.

Why do I mention this? Because I am going to explain to you why I have such an evil name. When I heard the answer, I said to myself: What can the god mean?[6] *And what is the interpretation of his riddle? For I know that I have no wisdom, small or great. What then can he mean when he says that I am the wisest of men? And yet he is a god, and cannot lie; that would be against his nature. After long consideration, I thought of a method of trying the questions. I reflected that if I could only find a man wiser than myself, then I might go to the god with a refutation in my hand. I should say to him, 'Here is a man who is wiser than I am; but you said that I was the wisest'. Accordingly I went to one who had a reputation of wisdom, and observed him – his name I need not mention, he was a politician whom I selected for examination – and the result was as*

---

[5] From Benjamin Jowett, *Apology: The Dialogues of Plato* Vol. 2 (3rd ed. Oxford: Clarendon, 1893). The passage is taken from paragraphs 20-22.

[6] Socrates believed that the god Apollo spoke through the medium of the Pythia (the priestess who represented the oracle).

follows. When I began to talk with him. I could not help thinking that he was not really wise, although he was thought wise by many, and still wiser by himself; and thereupon I tried to explain to him that he thought himself wise, but was not really wise; and the consequence was that he hated me, and his enmity was shared by several who were present and heard me. So I left him, saying to myself as I went away: Well, although I do not suppose that either of us knows anything really worth knowing, I am at least wiser than this fellow – for he knows nothing, and thinks that he knows; I neither know nor think that I know. In this latter particular, then, I seem to have slightly the advantage of him. Then I went to another who had still higher pretensions to wisdom, and my conclusion was exactly the same. Whereupon I made another enemy of him, and of many others besides him.

Then I went to one man after another, being not unconscious of the enmity which I provoked, and I lamented and feared this: but necessity was laid upon me, – the word of God, I thought, ought to be considered first. And I said to myself, Go I must to all who appear to know, and find out the meaning of the oracle. And I swear to you Athenians - by the dog I swear! - for I must tell you the truth – the result of my mission was just this: I found that the men most in repute were all but the most foolish; and that others less esteemed were really wiser and better. I will tell you the tale of my wanderings and of the 'Herculean' labours, as I may call them, which I endured only to find at last the oracle irrefutable. After the politicians, I went to the poets; tragic, dithyrambic, and all sorts. And there, I said to myself, you will be instantly detected; now you will find out that you are more ignorant than they are. Accordingly, I took some of the more elaborate passages in their writings, and asked what was the meaning of them - thinking that they would teach me something. Will you believe me? I am almost ashamed to confess the truth, but I must say that there is hardly a person present who would not have talked better about their poetry than they did themselves. Then I knew that not by wisdom do poets write poetry but by a sort of genius and inspiration; they are like diviners or soothsayers, who also say many fine things, but do not understand the meaning of them. The poets appeared to me to be much in the same case; and I further observed that upon the strength of their poetry they believed themselves to be the wisest of men in other things in which they were not wise. So I departed, conceiving myself to be superior to them for the same reason that I was superior to the politicians.

At last I went to the artisans, for I was conscious that I knew nothing at all, as I may say, and was sure that they knew many fine things; and here I was not mistaken, for they did know many things of which I was ignorant, and for this they were certainly wiser than I was. But I observed that even the good artisans fell into the same error as the poets; - because they were good workmen they thought that they also knew all sorts of other matters, and this defect in them overshadowed their wisdom; and therefore I asked myself on behalf of the oracle, whether I would like to be as I was, neither having their knowledge nor their ignorance, or like them in both; and I made answer to myself and to the oracle that I was better off as I was.

Question 1

In our day, is it still important to hear Socrates' claim: "The unexamined life is not worth living"? Was he right?

Comment

In this chapter I have suggested what Socrates was really claiming, but it may still be helpful to ponder how much his claim applies to our own, contemporary society.

Question 2

Is philosophy only taught in philosophy courses?

Comment

I suggest that the answer is "No". For example, when a good teacher of children, in a class on literature, asks whether a particular story or novel is "good", the children already are being asked to consider what makes one piece of writing better than another, and this invites critical thinking. Is a good novel one that tells an interesting story, or that portrays characters in a realistic way, or that encourages us and lifts our spirits, or that helps us to understand complex situations, or that promotes us to action (even if the novel is sad and makes us uncomfortable), or all of the above or none of the above? If I am right, philosophy, in the sense of critical thinking, quite often emerges during good teaching in ordinary schools.

Chapter 3. Plato and his Dialogues

Background

Whereas Socrates left no writings, Plato published a whole series of dialogues that were copied and recopied (by hand) many times both during his lifetime and ever since. Most of these have survived. His thought includes a strange mixture of authoritarian attitudes, especially in political matters, and individual liberty of thought, rooted in critical thinking. Part of his lasting legacy is a concern with how what is ethical is, in some way, interconnected with what is ultimately true. His concept of "The Idea of the Good" (in Greek *to agathon*) represents both what is ultimately most true and good, and what is beautiful. It has had a captivating effect on readers down to the present day.

1. Plato

Plato (c. 428-348 BCE) is the best-known of the pupils of Socrates. His dialogues were widely available in his lifetime and now form part of the Western philosophical canon. The 20th century philosopher, Alfred Whitehead, claimed that all subsequent European philosophy consisted of footnotes to Plato, and insofar as this is true we should take it to mean that Plato asked all (or most of) the great questions of philosophy, not that he *answered* them.

It is useful to divide the dialogues into three groups. The early ones, including the *Apology*, describe remembered conversations, and can be regarded as accounts of actual debates between Socrates and some of his pupils. No doubt these debates were somewhat reworked by Plato. In the middle period, we have the majority of his dialogues, including the *Republic*, where Socrates is the spokesperson, but the actual philosophy is clearly that of Plato. It is only loosely related to the actual teaching of Socrates. In the third period (for example, in the *Parmenides*), Plato begins to question much of his own teaching in previous dialogues, and sometimes all reference to Socrates is abandoned.

Being able to change one's mind, as Plato did, can be a sign of greatness rather than weakness, and we should note that several great philosophers changed their minds during the course of their lives.[1]

One of the dominant themes throughout the dialogues concerns what is referred to as *Idealism*. This refers not to "idealism", as when a person is said to have "ideals", but rather to Idea-ism, because of the central place in Plato's thought for what is called an Idea or a Form (*ideai* or *eide* in Greek). Here some explanation is needed. From the beginning, philosophers have been interested in what is called the problem of *universals* – the issue of how general terms (say "trees" or "horses") are related to individuals (such as "this tree" or "this horse"). Sometimes the contrast is described as that between *universals* and *particulars*. In later centuries the issue has tended to be seen more as a matter of words, or *semantics*, than of *ontology*, but it is important to appreciate how many ancient thinkers thought there was a real issue, perhaps mystery, here. The word *ontology* is used by philosophers to refer to questions concerning what is truly real – based on the Greek word for being or reality, *ontos*. What is it that makes all the different trees true examples of the same entity

---

[1] So we have to refer to their teaching as "at a certain period of their lives". In the 20th century Wittgenstein is a good example of this.

called *tree*? Plato's answer (one that he came to doubt later in his life) was that individual trees (or horses, or butterflies, or whatever) all get their essential nature from *participating* in an *Ideal* tree (or horse, butterfly, etc.), an Ideal that existed in an extra-sensory world. We are so accustomed to linking *reality* to things that can be experienced by our five senses that it is hard to enter the mindset of philosophers who thought that true reality was no such set of *objects*, but a matter of unseen realities that, as it were, lie behind them.

Interestingly, contemporary science, with its emphasis on subatomic particles that cannot be seen by our senses, may have more in common with such ancient ways of thinking than many people realize. For example, what binds all particular examples of (say) sulphur together is that they all "participate" in the essential element called sulphur. But this element is denoted, not by a material thing, but by an atomic number and the mathematical structure that comprises every atom of sulphur. Seen in this way, Plato's Ideas do not seem so fanciful.

Plato thought that some Ideas were higher, or more noble, than others, and at the pinnacle of this hierarchy was his "Idea of the Good" – a supreme moral principle that he sometimes referred to as "God".

Here, we must take care. At the time of Plato, all Greek was written in capitals, so that the distinction we sometimes make between *God* and *god* could not be made. As a result, in translating Plato, it is sometimes difficult to know whether to use a capital or a lower case "g". When Plato refers to "The Idea of the Good", which was for him supreme in the hierarchy of beings, there is a case for using the capital "G". However, although Plato's "Idea of the Good" was the closest thing in Plato's philosophy to the *God* of the Abrahamic religions, it is not the same. Plato's *God* is not a creator from nothing, nor even the "maker" of this world (out of pre-existing material) because this maker, which he called the *demiurge*, is another god-like being that ranks lower than the Idea of the Good. Moreover, neither the Idea of the Good nor the *demiurge* are "personal" (meaning being concerned with individual human persons and caring for them) – unlike the God of Judaism or Christianity or Islam.

In the dialogues Plato employs two principal techniques to present his position. The first is an argument, called *dialectic*. *Dialectic* is the normal Greek word for conversation, but for Plato (and probably for Socrates too) it acquired a technical meaning in which definition, or at least a description of a key term, is sought. In a typical dialogue the first suggestion is shown to be wrong, because it leads to a contradiction. The counter-argument that shows up the contradiction came, later on, to be referred to as an *antithesis*. A second definition is then offered, which, in turn, is shown to be deficient by another antithesis. Then a third definition is offered, and so on. The whole process will strike a familiar note for some readers because it can also be described as a *dialectical* movement. The process looks like this:

A. Thesis 1 – contradicted by Antithesis 1 – countered by Synthesis 1 (Synthesis 1 is a revised version of Thesis 1 that takes into account the objections of Antithesis 1).

B. Thesis 2 (which is identical to Synthesis 1) – contradicted by Antithesis 2 – countered by Synthesis 2 (a revised form of Thesis 2 that takes into account the objections of Antithesis 2).

C. Thesis 3 (which is identical to Synthesis 2) – and so on.

A good example of this dialectical method can be seen in Plato's dialogue called the *Theaetetus*. It begins with a search for an adequate account of true knowledge (*episteme*). In the dialogue

Definition 1 suggests: "knowledge is opinion". This is obviously wrong (Antithesis 1) because opinions vary while true knowledge must remain the same. Hence Definition 2 (which could be called Synthesis 1 or Thesis 2), which suggests: "knowledge is *true* opinion". This is better, but there is still a problem (Antithesis 2) because, as already suggested, if someone happens to have a true opinion, say by a lucky guess, this does not constitute "knowledge". Hence Definition 3 (which can be called Synthesis 2 or Thesis 3) that suggests: "knowledge is true opinion plus having good reasons (or a proof) that this opinion is true" (Plato says: "knowledge is true opinion plus *logos*" but *logos* can be taken here to mean good reason or proof). This is much better, and comes close to providing a good answer to the original question. However, Plato is still not ultimately satisfied, and he ends with the suggestion that we still have to search for a fuller answer.

There is an interesting explanation for why the dialogue ends without an absolute answer (and the same is true for most other dialogues). In the previous chapter we saw how Socrates claimed "that he knew that he knew nothing", and in the dialogues Plato is trying to be faithful to this general idea – and in particular to the suggestion that although human reason can make progress (Thesis 3 really is better than Thesis 1), we can never, in this life, reach absolute or full knowledge. Plato is being faithful to his master, Socrates.

Dialectic is the first technique, and the second – in contrast – is the use of myth (or allegory, or poetic image) to describe the truth as Plato sees it. Strictly speaking, this use of myth is not an appeal to rational *argument* at all, but it can be a powerful way of helping people to *understand* what has been suggested, and insofar as the picture that is presented seems to "ring true", we might say that there is, after all, an argument of a kind. We might say, for example, that the *Analects* of Confucius, or the Parables of Jesus, present pictures of what life is meant to be about that have a certain appeal, or evoke a sense of "resonance"; but it is only in this sense of resonance (quite unlike the logical or rational argument of the dialectic) that myth and parable and poetic image can point to "truth".

Let us turn to Plato's *Republic*, the most famous and influential of all his dialogues. It begins with a search for the meaning of justice (*to dikaion*), and by the use of dialectic it is shown that this cannot mean "the interest of the stronger" – which is the first definition or thesis that is offered, and which reflects a position commonly found among the Sophists. A modern view that is very similar claims "Might is Right", and Plato is fundamentally opposed to any such suggestion. "The Good" is an objective and ultimate reality that ought to guide all our actions, and it is quite different from what may happen to suit us, especially if we have a lust for power. During the following dialectic, the suggestion emerges that justice is some kind of harmony, in which there is a proper order, either within the state (for political justice) or within the individual (representing the virtue of justice within a good person). True virtue, and true justice, is a matter of having the right balance between the higher, or ruling elements (in either the state or the individual), and lower elements or passions.[2] There is

---

[2] When these "lower elements", such as our desire for comfort or fame, are treated as essentially bad, we have what later came to be called puritanism – in which such human strivings are classed in a purely negative way, and contrasted with the spiritual aspects of our nature. Although there may be some puritanical tendencies in Plato, he never took this extreme position. Bodily pleasures are not, for him, evil, only aspects of our nature that need to be kept under some control. Hence, the classical virtue of temperance. The same issue emerges in many religions. Jesus, for example, was certainly not a puritan in the sense of dismissing bodily pleasures (he enjoyed food and wine and good company), but – as in Plato – he taught that these things ought to be under the control of an overarching concern for the love of our neighbours.

then a long discussion concerning how the education of rulers (*the philosopher kings* who ought to be in charge of a just state) should be organized.

Plato's suggestions are fascinating, even though – most readers feel – totally impractical. Rooted in a kind of *meritocracy*, potentially gifted children (half of them girls)[3] are selected for a period of fifty years of careful training, after which they will be ready to take their place among the council of rulers. As objectors have pointed out from the beginning, this political philosophy is anything but democratic (which essentially means "rule by the people") and totally different from the Athenian democracy in which Plato grew up. But it is also quite different from most authoritarian systems because, allegedly, the fifty years of special education will guarantee that the rulers are both wise and benevolent. In his later writings, especially the *Laws*, Plato himself seems to have abandoned his defence of its practicality.[4]

---

[3] Plato's suggestion that in an ideal state women should have equality with men, as far as rulership is concerned, is extraordinary, given the nearly universal assumption of the superiority of males in the ancient world.

[4] An historical incident may have contributed to Plato's change of mind. He was asked to educate the son of a dictator at Syracuse, and this may have seemed like an opportunity to educate a boy so that he could become a philosopher king. The boy and/or the system of education did not turn out well, and this experience, some think, contributed to Plato's decision that his proposed educational system could not be made to work in the real world.

A reading from Plato's *Republic*.

At the climax of the *Republic* Plato turns from dialectical argument to the presentation of a myth, generally known as "the Allegory of the Cave". Here is its core:[5]

And now, I said, let me show in a figure how far our nature is enlightened or unenlightened: -- Behold! Human beings housed in an underground den, which has a mouth open towards the light and reaching all along the den; here they have been from their childhood, and have their legs and necks chained, so that they cannot move and can only see before them, being prevented by the chains from turning round their heads. Above and behind them a fire is blazing at a distance, and between the fire and the prisoners there is a raised way; and you will see, if you look, a low wall built along the way, like the screen which marionette players have in front of them, over which they show the puppets.

I see.

And do you see, I said, men passing along the wall carrying all sorts of vessels, and statues and figures of animals made of wood and stone and various materials, which appear over the wall? While carrying their burdens, some of them, as you would expect, are talking, others silent.

You have shown me a strange image, and they are strange prisoners.

Like ourselves, I replied; and they see only their own shadows, or the shadows of one another, which the fire throws on the opposite wall of the cave?

True, he said; how could they see anything but the shadows if

---

[5] Book VII, paragraphs 514-517. This passage is from Benjamin Jowett: *The Republic* (3rd ed. Oxford: Clarendon Press, 1883). This edition is widely available online, including from Project Gutenberg.

they were never allowed to move their heads?

And of the objects which are being carried in like manner they would only see the shadows?

Yes, he said.

And if they were able to converse with one another, would they not suppose that they were naming what was actually before them?

Very true.

And suppose further that the prison had an echo which came from the other side, would they not be sure to fancy when one of the passers-by spoke that the voice which they heard came from the passing shadows?

No question, he replied.

To them, I said, the truth would be literally nothing but the shadows of the images.

That is certain.

And now look again, and see what will naturally follow if the prisoners are released and disabused of their error. At first, when any of them is liberated and compelled suddenly to stand up and turn his neck round and walk and look towards the light, he will suffer sharp pains; the glare will distress him, and he will be unable to see the realities of which in his former state he had seen the shadows; and then conceive someone saying to him that what he saw before was an illusion, but that now, when he is approaching nearer to being and his eye is turned towards more real existence, he has a clearer vision, – what will be his reply? And you may further imagine that his instructor is pointing to the objects as they pass and requiring him to name them – will he not be perplexed? Will he not fancy that the shadows which he formerly saw are truer than the objects which are now shown to him?

Far truer.

And if he is compelled to look straight at the light, will he not have a pain in his eyes which will make him turn away to take refuge in the objects of vision which he can see, and which he will conceive to be in reality clearer than the things which are now being shown to him?

True, he said.

And suppose once more, that he is reluctantly dragged up a steep and rugged ascent, and held fast until he is forced into the presence of the sun himself, is he not likely to be pained and irritated? When he approaches the light his eyes will be dazzled, and he will not be able to see anything at all of what are now called realities.

Not all in a moment, he said.

He will require to grow accustomed to the sight of the upper world. And first he will see the shadows best, next the reflections of men and other objects in the water, and then the objects themselves; then he will gaze upon the light of the moon and the stars and the spangled heaven; and he will see the sky and the stars by night better than the sun or the light of the sun by day?

Certainly.

Last of all he will be able to see the sun, and not mere reflections of him in the water, but he will see him in his own proper place, and not in another; and he will contemplate him as he is.

Certainly.

He will then proceed to argue that this is he who gives the seasons and the years, and is the guardian of all that is in the visible world, and in a certain way the cause of all things which he and his followers have been accustomed to behold?

Clearly, he said, he would first see the sun and then reason about him.

And when he remembered his old habitation, and the wisdom of the den and his fellow-prisoners, do you not suppose that he would felicitate himself on the change, and pity them?

Certainly, he would.

And if they were in the habit of conferring honours among themselves on those who were quickest to observe the passing shadows and to remark which of them went before, and which followed after, and which were together; and who were the best able to draw conclusions as to the future, do you think that he would care for such honours and glories, or envy the possessors of them? Would he not say with Homer,

'Better to be the poor servant of a poor master'

and to endure anything, rather than think as they do and live after their manner?

Yes, he said, I think he would rather suffer anything than entertain these false notions and live in this miserable manner.

Imagine once more, I said, such an one coming down suddenly out of the sun and being replaced in his old seat; would he not be certain to have his eyes full of darkness?

To be sure, he said.

And if there were a contest, and he had to compete in measuring the shadows with the prisoners who had never moved out of the den, while his sight was still weak, and before his eyes had become steady (and the time which would be needed to acquire this new habit of sight might be very considerable), would he not be ridiculous? Men would say of him that up he went and down he came without his eyes; and that it was better not even to think of ascending; and if anyone tried to loose another and lead him up to the light, let them only catch the offender, and they would put him to death.

No question, he said.

This entire allegory, I said, you may now append, dear Glaucon, to the previous argument; the prison-house is the world of sight, the light of the fire is the sun, and you will not misapprehend me if you interpret the journey upwards to be the ascent of the soul into the intellectual world according to my poor belief, which, at your desire, I have expressed – whether rightly or wrongly God knows. But, whether true or false, my opinion is that in the world of knowledge the idea of good appears last of all, and is seen only with an effort; and, when seen, is also inferred to be the universal author of all things beautiful and right, parent of light and of the lord of light in the visible world, and the immediate source of reason and truth in the intellectual; and that this is the power upon which he who would act rationally either in public or private life must have his eye fixed.

Several comments can be made on this famous passage that has been of such huge influence in Western philosophy.

1. Note how Plato calls to mind the person of Socrates, who was put to death for trying to lead his students towards the light.

2. The objects outside the cave – in the "real" world – are the Ideas, and the supreme example of these Ideas is the Idea of the Good.

3. The shadows which the prisoners see on the back wall are not even copies of the original, they are "copies of copies" – at least two stages removed from true reality.

Not only is a philosophy implicit in all of this (it is an example of metaphysics[6]) – there is also a kind of moral vocation or calling. Our duty, on this earth, is to ascend up towards the real world and eventually gaze at the true light. It is also our duty and our calling to help others to do the same, and to lead an examined life, even though (as with Socrates) this may put our mortal lives in danger.

---

[6] The origin and meaning of metaphysics was discussed in the first chapter (see note 7). In Aristotle's book of that name he discusses ultimate questions, especially how the whole universe is kept in motion by a supreme principle that he calls God and describes as "the

Question 1

Was Plato naive to think (in the middle period of his life) that even a perfect education would guarantee that a person would end up "good"?

Comment

Plato claimed: "virtue is knowledge". If "knowledge" is thought of as knowing a lot of facts, Plato would seem to be wrong (because all sorts of people who are both clever and well-informed can still be bad). Perhaps he meant by "knowledge" something rather different, some kind of spiritual knowledge. However, if this is so, it is difficult to see how any system of education or training could guarantee that this would be achieved.

Question 2

Was Plato right to assume that ultimate reality has the characteristic of goodness? According to Plato the Idea of the Good is the supreme reality.

Comment

This is an issue that sharply divides philosophers. Those who embrace one of the world's great religions agree with this Platonic belief. Is this a "belief", or for Plato, something he thinks he has proved? Many secular thinkers believe that there is no ultimate relationship between what is ultimately true and what is ultimately good – because what we call good is purely a matter of human

---

first unmoved mover". As with Plato's Idea of the Good, this "God" is not concerned with the life of individual humans, but – perhaps surprisingly – according to Aristotle, he (or it) does have at least one personal characteristic, because his God is *happy* (since he is wrapped up in his own eternal, mathematical thoughts).

desires and emotions, with no fundamental relationship with what is true. The human world, ultimately, according to them, may be basically tragic. However, a number of purely secular philosophers believe in moral truths (such as the intrinsic dignity of all persons), so the issue is more complicated than it might appear.

In fact, Plato thought that three fundamental concepts were interlinked: the good and the true and the beautiful. This invites all kinds of questions about the nature of art, and its possible relationship to ethics or truth, which go beyond the scope of this book.

Chapter 4. Aristotle's virtue ethics

Background

Whereas most of Plato's dialogues have survived, none of those written by Aristotle has, except for some fragments. Instead, by a strange quirk of fortune, some of what may have been his lecture notes have survived. There is an ancient story to the effect that these treatises or notes were rediscovered in a damp cellar in the first century BCE. Some of this material has been referred to as Aristotle's *treatises*, but it is unlikely that they were intended for publication in the form in which we have them. This helps to explain the very different style of his works, compared with those of Plato, and also introduces the problem that sometimes we don't know whether the notes express his own opinions or those that he is discussing (although the context often makes this clear).

1. Aristotle

Plato was the most famous pupil of Socrates, and Aristotle (c. 384-322 BCE) the most famous pupil of Plato. Interestingly, Alexander the Great was the most famous pupil of Aristotle, but Alexander was not a philosopher and the importance of his connection with Aristotle is simply the fact that Alexander's conquests helped spread Greek culture across much of Asia. Before focusing on Aristotle's moral philosophy, we should note two aspects of his more general philosophy that impact on his ethics.

First, he came to reject Plato's theory of Ideas, holding that they represented an unnecessary duplication of reality. He argued that the only things that existed, as *substances*, were the objects themselves. Nevertheless, the *universal* had a kind of *reality*, a pattern or form that the scientist can study. Second – and related to this emphasis on individual substances – Aristotle introduced a strong element of what we call *empiricism* into his philosophy, that is to say, a stress on systematic observation, by the five senses, of sensory reality. Later this systematic observation turned into what we now regard as scientific methodology, which includes not only systematic observation and measurement, but also the framing of hypotheses that lead to predictions, and then either the verification or falsification of these predictions by experiment and observation. Acting as a biologist, Aristotle collected, dissected and classified varieties of fish. He also sent out his students to make an empirical study of some 150 constitutions in other city-states. Here we see an early example of the type of political science that is an empirical study of how states actually work, in contrast with the ethical issue of how they *ought* to work. Aristotle was a political scientist in both senses.

Few of Aristotle's followers showed the same interest in empirical evidence, preferring either mathematical rationality or speculative metaphysics. Had they taken up the empirical aspect of Aristotle's thought, the history of the world might have been very different, with the flowering of the empirical sciences not having to wait until around 1600. However, some philosophers of science think that the empirical sciences could not really have taken off without important advances in technology – such as the invention of the telescope at the time of Galileo – so this matter is hotly debated.

Turning to Aristotle's ethics, it may be helpful to put this in a wider context. Modern students of moral philosophy are often taught that there are three main types of this philosophy: utilitarianism – which we shall examine in chapter 9; deontology – which we shall examine in chapter 10; and *virtue ethics* – which is said to begin with Aristotle. In fact this is very misleading, because there are lots of reputable theories of ethics that do not fit any of these three categories; and Aristotle, while underlining the importance of virtue, was not the first to do so. However, his views have been extremely influential and most accounts of virtue ethics begin with them. An account of human virtue forms the core of his ethical teaching. There are two Greek words translated as "virtue", *arete* and *hexis*. *Arete* is the more general term, but *hexis*, in my view, is the more interesting, because he defines this as an acquired human disposition. In contrast, a "natural virtue" (*arete*) could be the happy accident of being born with a gentle disposition (we might say as a result of the genes we had at birth). We might praise a person for this natural disposition, but it is not, strictly speaking, the kind of moral praise that we would be likely to bestow on someone who acquired temperance, by a long struggle in which they developed the habit of acting with temperance – for example, by resisting temptations to act rashly. We might say that praising someone for a good character that resulted from their genes was rather like praising someone for having a beautiful pair of eyes. For Aristotle, the goal of life, and equally the purpose of a good education, is the development of virtue, especially *hexeis* (the plural of *hexis*). This will lead, in most cases, to happiness or wellbeing. Once again, Aristotle's position is more subtle and more interesting than at first sight, especially when he considers the relationship between the Greek words *eudaimonia* (usually translated as happiness or wellbeing) and *hedone* (usually translated as pleasure and the root of the English word *hedonism*.) The overall purpose of intelligent life, Aristotle argues, is to pursue happiness (*eudaimonia*). This is the final end (Greek *telos*) of human life, but rather than implying a crass accumulation of pleasure, instead it is a life full of all kinds of good things. These include friendship and the virtuous actions that we all have the capacity for. Happiness, although the ultimate end of human life, is a by-product of living well – and the virtues are the clue to how we can do that.

One of the indications that seeking happiness, although an ultimate end, is also more than a selfish search for personal pleasure, is found in Aristotle's long discussion of friendship (*philia* in Greek). In its highest form,[1] friendship sees the friend as an alter ego (Latin for "another self") – a person whose happiness one treasures for its own sake and not for what we can gain from it. Here, once again, we see that personal happiness is a kind of by-product of virtue, rather than a selfish quest.

In our day it is common to contrast the selfish life, in which people neglect virtue for the sake of personal satisfaction, and the morally good life, which may not lead to personal happiness. This is because it often means giving up many things that we want, including power and success. Both Plato and Aristotle saw things differently, so that there was an inevitable interconnection between the moral life, when properly pursued, and long-term happiness. The person who seeks personal satisfaction above all else gets caught up in a kind of spiral that inevitably, in the long run, leads not to the happiness that is sought, but to some kind of caricature of the good life.[2] The truly

---

[1] Aristotle discusses three levels of friendship: the first for pleasure, the second for utility (as in business relationships), the third – and highest – for sharing common goods. Nowhere could it be clearer that personal selfishness is not what life is really about.

[2] Similarly, in the *Republic*, Plato argues that those who seek power rather than the good end up so damaging their souls that they are not capable of real, long-term happiness.

good life, one with genuine and lasting pleasures (such as those that result from genuine friendship) can only come as a result of a virtuous life. However, Aristotle insists that this is only true when we take life as a whole. In the short term, acting virtuously may often lead to pain, danger, and even death. In the face of death, Aristotle believed in a kind of immortality, but unlike Plato, it consisted only of the intellectual component of our souls, which he calls *nous*.

The notion of immortality illustrates, yet again, the need for critical thinking, because the term can mean very different things.

For both Plato and the mainstream Abrahamic religions, immortality means the continuance of the person, or at least of a kind of "central core". (All religions acknowledge the need for some kind of transformation of the self, especially of its egoistic side.) At the other extreme we find belief in the total annihilation of the self, both in some schools of Buddhism and – for different reasons – in much contemporary secular thought. In between we have many philosophical positions in which certain elements of the self are preserved, in the case of Aristotle of what he called *nous*, a kind of intellectual element that he separated from all personal desires. We shall find further examples of such notions in both Stoicism and Neoplatonism.

Central to Aristotle's view of the relationship of the self to others is a philosophy of nature – a typically Greek belief – that the world that we humans inhabit is subject to laws and patterns written into the fabric of the universe. There is what some commentators have described as a "great chain of being", a kind of hierarchy in which the higher elements of the cosmos are intrinsically more advanced and more noble than those lower down the chain. To put this in another way, the order of reality is, at the same time, *both* a kind of description of what things truly are, and an evaluation of how precious things really are. Here there is a huge contrast with the way many philosophers now see things (with no intimate connection between what is good and what is true)[3] – but if we are to appreciate Aristotle, we have at least to enter sympathetically into his thought, even if we go on to reject them.

For Aristotle the great chain of being goes like this:

1. Prime matter (the lowest element in the great chain and the material out of which all physical things are made).

2. Vegetables, which have a kind of soul – *psyche* in Greek – which represents the organizing principle of vegetable life. Here we have organisms in which the inter-relationship of the parts (unlike a pile of stones) is *constitutive* of what an organic being is.

3. Animals – which have *sensitive* as well as vegetative souls.

4. Human beings – which have *rational* as well as vegetative and sensitive souls.

5. Spiritual beings.

Levels 2-5 have further hierarchies built into them. For example, in the case of humans, Aristotle thought that Greeks were superior to other races, and men to women. Similarly, there is a hierarchy within the order of spiritual realities. Where, at the top, Plato has the Idea of the Good, Aristotle has the "first unmoved mover" that caused all forms of motion. In his *Metaphysics* he argues that all the lower elements are "moved" by love (*eros*); but the pinnacle of the hierarchy, although the cause of all movement, is itself unmoved.

---

[3] Since the time of the Scottish philosopher David Hume, this has been known either as the "is/ought" or as the "fact/value" distinction. Whether or not we are right to make absolute distinctions of this kind, it is important to enter into the mindset of Greek philosophers who saw the two aspects (i.e. facts and values) as intimately connected. This is part of what Plato meant when he saw the good, the true and the beautiful as being intimately bound together.

Although this "God" is very different from that of the Abrahamic religions, Aristotle's view has fed into the notion that their God is also necessarily changeless and unmoved.

It is easy for us to find fault with this great chain of being, especially in the kind of elitism that places one race above another, or men above women, or that places those born as aristocrats above those in other classes. I imagine that almost all readers will share my rejection of these three suggestions. We can add the point that – contrary to Aristotle – we now know that many non-human animals have certain rational capacities. However, this does not mean that we should reject the whole system completely. For example, most of us do think that the life and interests of human beings are more important than those of non-human animals, even if we value animal life and seek an environmental philosophy that protects it. Further, rightly or wrongly, we tend to have more regard for (say) mammals than (say) mosquitos – so that we often think and act with some such hierarchy in mind. Similarly we find no difficulty in the idea of animals eating vegetables. Many details of the hierarchy are clearly wrong, but – in general terms – it often resonates with how we view the world. We should also note how the very idea of a great chain of being resonates with Socrates' claim that "the unexamined life is not worth living". What life is really about is not just indulging in the animal parts of our nature,[4] but finding and enabling and growing the "higher" elements. Here, as already suggested, there is a kind of elitism, but it is one that we might be happy to defend. It does not (or should not) mark a distinction between classes of people, but

---

[4] Plato and Aristotle never took the step of saying that these "lower" elements are bad (as do certain forms of puritanism), rather they had their proper place and function within the good life. However, they had to be under the rule of the higher elements. The virtue of maintaining this proper order was what they meant by temperance.

it should mark a distinction – for all people – between a sluggardly life, and one full of intellectual vigour, artistic enterprise, and rich relationships with other people.

Virtues then are human dispositions that characterize how we tend to act, usually instinctively, as a result of the characters we have gradually developed. This is helpful, because although sometimes it is good to stop and ponder how to respond to a situation, it would be impossible to do this most of the time. Instead we just act naturally in accordance with our character. Further, according to Aristotle, each virtue is a kind of mean. For example, courage is a compromise between the extremes of rashness on the one side and timidity on the other.

In this brief overview of Aristotle's ethics, there are three other considerations that need to be stressed.

First, he contrasts what he calls "natural" with "conventional" justice. Some things are held to be right and wrong only within certain cultures. This is conventional justice and Aristotle has no problem in accepting that this is quite properly the case. At the same time, he insists that *some* ethical standards are *universal*. It is easy to misunderstand what he means by this. He does not mean that we will always *find* these universal standards wherever we look. He means instead that they are standards we *ought to find* if people are truly to flourish.[5] The universality is one that needs to be discovered and enacted if we are to fulfil our proper places within the great chain of being. For example, every culture ought to promote courage and honesty in its citizens because bravery and integrity are "natural" and

---

[5] Aristotle denies that natural justice is absolute in the sense of allowing no variation at all. The point is rather that it relates to what will fulfil our potentialities rather than to what a particular culture happens to promote, as in conventions.

necessary to the completion or fulfilment of all human beings, but there is no reason why there should not be purely local rules on (say) what dress code we ought to follow.

Second, in Aristotle's ethics there is a useful discussion of the difference between *voluntary* and *involuntary* action. We only blame people, or at least, we ought only to blame people, for actions that are *voluntary* – and basically this means, he argues, that the source of movement comes from *within* the person. Thus, if I am pushed into the path of an oncoming cyclist, it is not I who am responsible, but the person who pushed me. However, if I wander carelessly into the path of an oncoming cyclist, the source of movement comes from within me, not another person, so I am responsible for what happens. In an important addition, Aristotle discusses the situations that arise when people act "in ignorance", and the point he makes is of crucial importance, not only for how we frame our moral judgments, but also for how any humane system of law ought to work. Basically, if I am responsible for that ignorance, either because I was careless, or just didn't bother to find out what was going on, then I am responsible for my actions. I am therefore guilty even if, at the time of the action, I acted "in ignorance". However, if I am misled, or deceived by a hoax, then I am not responsible for my ignorance. Similarly, if I choose to get drunk and then commit some awful crime, I am responsible, and can properly be found guilty. However, if someone forcibly pours alcohol down my throat, or pretends that he is serving lemonade instead of gin (and I am too inexperienced to note the difference), then the drunkenness is the result of the other person's actions; it does not come from "within me".[6]

---

[6] In modern legal systems, acting in the kind of ignorance that Aristotle says makes one responsible, while not exonerating a person, might count as a mitigating circumstance and affect the punishment that ought to be due.

We should note that Aristotle's discussion of this is only tangential to the contemporary issue of free will. The contemporary issue centres on whether we can distinguish two kinds of action, *both* of which arise from "within" my brain; one that can be freely chosen; and one that is solely caused by (say) some abnormality within the structure of the brain. We shall revisit this important issue later in the book.

Third, there is an influential discussion of what Aristotle calls *akrasia*, usually translated as "weakness of the will". Superficially, there is a huge contrast here with Plato, because when Plato said that "virtue is knowledge", or (as a consequence of this) "no-one knowingly does evil", it would seem that wrongdoing is merely the result of not understanding or not knowing the issues. However, this is a good example of where, if we do some critical thinking, we can see that what we mean by "knowing" has to be examined more carefully. When we engage in critical thinking we see that the difference between Plato and Aristotle is not nearly as sharp as it first looks. For example, in Plato's Allegory of the Cave, when the released prisoners come to understand and "know" that the things they had thought to be real were mere copies or images, this is not simple *factual* knowledge, such as knowing that I live in house number 19. It is much more like that kind of "knowledge" we have when someone "comes to know" they are loved by their parents. Usually, a word like "understand" or "realize" or "comprehend" would be just as appropriate as "know". Aristotle is clearly right to say that we can have factual knowledge, even that a certain course of action is, in some way, wrong, but then – through weakness of will – fail to perform it.[7] In highlighting this, he marks a genuine problem, perhaps one that Plato tends to neglect, but the difference is less stark than might appear.

When, in the dialogue called the *Phaedrus*, Plato describes the human soul as being guided by two horses – one white and noble, the other dark and ignoble – he shows sensitivity to the ambivalent passions and emotions that drive us. Our passions and emotions, like the two horses, tend to pull us in different directions and it is up to the charioteer (perhaps representing our overall rationality) to guide the whole chariot. One of the questions that arises is this: Within the model that Plato provides, how is the charioteer himself or herself moved to favour one horse rather than another?

A reading from Aristotle's *Nichomachean Ethics*, Book 3.i.2-6[8]

It is then generally held that actions are involuntary when done (a) under compulsion or (b) through ignorance; and that (a) an act is compulsory when its origin is from without, being of such a nature that the agent, who is really passive, contributes nothing to it; for example, when he is carried somewhere by

---

[7] For Christians this issue is highlighted by the notion of the human race having *fallen*. For conservative Christians this fall refers to an actual *historical* fall (at the time of Adam and Eve); for many contemporary Christians it refers not to an historical event, but (through the use of a myth or parable based on the story of Adam and Eve) to a psychological truth about the human condition. Because of our evolutionary past, both individually and socially, we suffer from a kind of moral weakness. In the Orthodox (and Eastern) traditions of Christianity, the stress has always been on an inborn moral *weakness*, and not on inborn *guilt* (Latin *culpa*) – which many Western churches have tended to stress.

[8] All passages are based on the translation by H. Rackham (Cambridge, Mass: Loeb, 1926).

stress of weather, or by people who have him in their power. But there is some doubt about actions done through fear of a worse alternative, or for some noble object – as for instance if a tyrant having a man's parents and children in his power commands him to do something base, when if he complies their lives will be spared but if he refuses they will be put to death. It is open to question whether such actions are voluntary or involuntary. A somewhat similar case is when cargo is jettisoned in a storm; apart from circumstances, no one voluntarily throws away his property, but to save his own life and that of his shipmates any sane man would do so. Acts of this kind, then, are 'mixed' or composite; but they approximate rather to the voluntary class. For at the actual time they are done they are chosen or willed; and the end or motive of an act varies with the occasion, so that the terms 'voluntary' and 'involuntary' should be used with reference to the time of action...

Comment

Although there are sometimes clear cases of acting in a voluntary or involuntary manner, Aristotle helps us to see how some cases fall, as it were, between the two.

A reading from Book 5.vii.1-3

Political justice is of two kinds, one natural, the other conventional. A rule of justice is natural that has the same validity everywhere, and does not depend on our accepting it or not. A rule is conventional that in the first instance may be settled in one way or the other indifferently, though having once been settled it is not indifferent; for example, that the ransom for a prisoner shall be a mina, that a sacrifice shall consist of a goat and not of two sheep;

and any regulation enacted for particular cases, for instance the sacrifice in honour of Brasidas, and ordinances in the nature of special decrees. Some people think that all rules of justice are merely conventional, because, whereas a law of nature is immutable and has the same validity everywhere, as fire burns both here and in Persia, rules of justice are seen to vary. That rules of justice vary is not absolutely true, but only with qualifications. Among the gods indeed it is perhaps not true at all; but in our world, although there is such a thing as Natural Justice, all rules of justice are variable.

Comment

In our day a traffic rule, such as "In the U.K. you must drive on the left side of the road", is a clear example of what Aristotle calls "conventional justice" – reached by agreement. Once the agreement has been reached, it is obviously important for all to follow it, even though there was no original reason for the choice of left rather than right. Many of the Sophists (against whom, as we have seen, Socrates and Plato argued) claimed that all justice was merely conventional. Socrates, Plato and Aristotle all disputed this. Some matters (such as bringing up children to have the virtues of temperance and courage) are *universally* required if they (and society) are to flourish.

A reading from Book 7.ii.1-2

How can a man fail in self-restraint when believing correctly that what he does is wrong? Some people say that he cannot do so when he knows the act to be wrong; since, as Socrates held, it would be strange if, when a man possessed Knowledge, some other thing should overpower it, and 'drag it about like a slave.' In fact Socrates used to combat the view altogether, implying that there is no such thing as Unrestraint, since no one, he held, acts contrary to what is best, believing what he does to be bad, but only through ignorance.

Now this theory is manifestly at variance with plain facts…

Comment

As the earlier discussion has indicated, I hold that Aristotle is not altogether fair to Socrates here. If we take knowledge in a very general sense Aristotle makes a fair point – for there does seem to be a glaring contradiction with how some people behave. However, if we consider the different senses of "knowing" the issue soon becomes more ambiguous.

Question 1

Why does Aristotle believe that some human beings are intrinsically more noble than others?

Comment

If we believe that all human beings have an (equal) intrinsic dignity, can we frame a counter-argument to Aristotle? Does this counter-argument appeal to metaphysics in some way, or is it purely based on an appeal to our feelings?

Question 2

Is Aristotle right to distinguish happiness from pleasure?

Comment

We shall revisit this question in the chapter on utilitarianism.

Question 3

Is Aristotle's account of voluntary and involuntary action absolutely necessary if we are to have a workable criminal law?

Comment

In the modern era, most systems of criminal law allow an "insanity defence", so it is no longer the case that the law treats all actions that originate from within a person as the same. When the cause of our actions originates within the human brain (or mind) can we distinguish (i) those that are really "free" from (ii) those that are determined and (iii) those that are random?

A comment on the equality of women

Although some ancient cultures ranked women highly, this has been the exception, and Aristotle's view, or some variation of it, has been common. Plato, as we noted, was exceptional in suggesting that half the philosopher rulers should be women. (Also, the prophetic figure whose wisdom helps Socrates in Plato's *Symposium*, is the woman, Diotima.) Although there is controversy concerning whether the founders of the great religions supported male dominance, there is little doubt that most religions have practised it, at least until recent times. Interesting exceptions include the Quakers, who have had virtually identical male and female leadership from around 1650, the teaching of early Sikhism, and the Japanese religion known as Tenrikyo, founded by a women prophet, Nakayama Miki (1799-1889). In our day, those who still support something akin to Aristotle's hierarchy tend to argue like this: "Women and men are equal but different. Just as only women can bear children, so their roles, while of equal value, are different." At first glance this claim may seem to make sense, but as soon as we expose it to critical thinking we find that what most exponents actually mean is that men are more suited to *leadership* roles. My own view is that any fair-minded empirical study shows that this is not so. Given opportunity in politics, business, religious organizations, etc., there may be evidence that the role played by women tends to be slightly *different* or complementary, but not less efficient or beneficial. We see how careful we have to be with this word "different". I suggest that this is one of many areas where the application of critical thinking leads to a definite conclusion in practical ethics – a conclusion against any version of Aristotelian discrimination.

Chapter 5. Stoics, Epicureans and the emergence of Christian moral philosophy (with special reference to Origen and Augustine)

Background

In its early years Christianity was a relatively small religious movement, or sect, strongly associated with Judaism, and persecuted by some of the Roman emperors. With the conversion of the Emperor Constantine to Christianity, about 312 CE, slowly things began to change. Some of Constantine's successors continued to persecute the Christians. But gradually, a "Christendom" emerged in which the Roman Empire and Christianity became intermingled in terms of law and political influence. Whether this was a good thing or a bad thing – for either state or church – is hotly debated. Some argue that it led to the corruption of both institutions, others that it led to progress. Whatever the truth of this matter, until the time of Hobbes (the subject of chapter 7) Western moral philosophy was dominated by Christian philosophers, and this is why religion will feature so much both in this chapter – which outlines the gradual development of Christian philosophy – and the next, in which we will focus on the thought of Thomas Aquinas, the most influential of all Christian philosophers after Augustine.

1. Philosophy after Plato and Aristotle

In the next chapter we shall be looking at the kind of Christian philosophy that dominated the European Middle Ages, and that still holds considerable influence in many parts of the world. In this chapter we shall examine four of the dominant philosophies (in addition to those of Plato and Aristotle) that provide the background for this Christian philosophy, without which it would be hard to understand where it came from and what it claimed.

2. Epicureanism

In ancient Greece there emerged four principal "schools" of philosophy: Plato's was known as the Academy. Aristotle's was known as the Lyceum[1]. The Epicureans were associated with a garden in which the members often met. The Stoics were named after the Stoa (the Greek word for a porch or covered walkway) where they often gathered. However, it must be remembered that there were also many Greek philosophers who did not belong to any of these four schools and some of them, such as Heraclitus, have been exceedingly influential. Epicurus (c. 341-270 BCE) the founder of the Epicurean school, was one of Plato's rivals, but he was not aligned with Plato's principal opponents, the Sophists. As with many philosophers, Epicurus' view of ethics was intimately related to his metaphysics (his theory of ultimate reality). He was an exponent of what would later be called *materialism*, partly because of his belief in the atomic theory of matter, which was seen as being in direct opposition to Plato's Idealism. Instead of invisible Ideas providing the stuff of ultimate reality, it was these tiny objects, called atoms, out of which all things were formed. Consistently, Epicurus held that

---

[1] Also known as the Peripatetic school because, apparently, Aristotle used to walk around as he taught, and peripatetic is the Greek word for this movement.

even the gods (whom he thought did exist) – and who like us, were made out of atoms – were not beings to be worshipped. He not only doubted the wild stories about these gods (as did Socrates and Plato), but he also denied they had any interest in human affairs. His moral philosophy was designed, in part, to free us from any concern with gods or God. The presence of human suffering – he held – showed that the gods or God could not be both all-powerful and benign. The proper way to live, said Epicurus, is to recognize the irrelevance of the gods and to be as happy as possible. However, contrary to what is sometimes said about Epicureans, this did not mean that he advocated an extravagant "eat, drink and be merry" approach to the pleasures that we should seek. Even though the "wise man" seeks the maximization of his pleasure, he strongly advocates moderation, and the virtues that make for this approach to life. In particular, the "wise man" would seek a "serenity of the soul". Only by such moderation are we likely to live long and happy lives. For similar reasons, Epicurus strongly supported genuine friendships. This is one of the paradoxes of Epicurean philosophy (and perhaps all moral philosophies are subject to some paradoxes). The ultimate reason for cultivating friendship, according to Epicurean philosophy, is our own long-term pleasure, and yet, at the same time, this philosophy recognizes that genuine friendship involves the development of unselfish affection.

3. Stoicism

The founder of Stoicism was Zeno (c. 336-264 BCE) of Citium, a city in Cyprus. The school, in various forms, had a longer history than the others, in part because of its appeal to the Romans. As so often in philosophy, the ethical teaching has an intimate link with the more general metaphysics. For most Stoics, God (and here the capital is appropriate) was not a personal being who was interested in individual humans, but was the great Fire, or great Reason, and we – as individual centres of intelligence – are akin to sparks of the great Fire, or fragments of this universal Reason. When we die, we merge with this great Fire, from which we came. So there is an immortality of a kind, but not – at least according to most Stoics – a personal, individual immortality. This belief or philosophy has much in common with certain Eastern schools of philosophy and religion that go under the general name of monism (from the Greek word for "one" or "oneness"), in which all elements of personal individuality are ultimately illusory. Eternal life is, in a way, guaranteed, but it is not an eternal life for the person that we think of as you or me. To use a frequent metaphor, it is like a drop of water returning to the ocean from which it came.

The ethical teaching that comes from this philosophy is one in which we seek to suppress our individual desires and passions in favour of virtuous characters and virtuous acts that (i) support the wider community and (ii) help prepare us for our eventual integration with God. This is precisely the kind of ethics that makes for good soldiers (at least if we neglect any possible responsibility of the soldiers to question the rightness of the cause for which they fight), and thus helps to explain the attraction of this kind of ethic for many of the Roman leaders who depended so much on the success of their army.

At least superficially, there is a resemblance between this Stoic ethic, in which our personal desires are secondary to our social duties, and Buddhist ethics. For Buddhism, the way to overcome suffering is to avoid "attachment" (*trishna* in Sanskrit) and to develop "detachment", so that although we should work to reduce the suffering of others, the more spiritually advanced we are the

Stoics, Epicureans and the emergence of Christian moral philosophy

less we are personally *affected* by suffering – either of others or of ourselves. Here, great care is needed if we are to be faithful to the spirit of critical inquiry, because the word *trishna* can be rendered as "craving" as well as "desiring", and the proper way to understand Buddhist ethics requires a careful examination of exactly what kind of detachment is called for, and equally, how far the similarity with Stoic ethics is superficial or profound.

The issue, in terms of how we should show compassion, but not – in a sense – be *affected* by our compassion, can be brought out by reference to the teaching of the famous Stoic philosopher Epictetus (c. 50-138 CE), who began life as a slave. One of his famous teachings was that when we see suffering, we should groan alongside the one who suffers – if in this way we can help the sufferer – but when we do this, "do not groan inwardly". One, somewhat loose translation goes: "Sigh, but do not sigh with the heart".[2] This is an interesting difference with the way most people understand the idea of love, especially in the sense of *agape* (the Greek word for "love" in the New Testament). Love certainly involves acting for the good of others, but on most accounts, it also includes *feelings* of affection, so that (as St. Paul put it) "we rejoice with them that rejoice and weep with those who weep".

The works of Epictetus make for great reading, and often provide valuable advice on how to live in this world. His frequent expressions of devotion to God (or Zeus) can easily give the impression that he is closer to theism (belief in a personal God) than to monism (which is more like the official position of Stoicism). However, it is probable that these expressions of devotion are more indicative of a personal attraction to the notion of *goodness* than

---

[2] Epictetus, *Enchiridion* 16.

affection for a personal deity.[3]

Another feature of Stoic ethics is the emphasis on what is termed "cosmopolitanism" – from the Greek word, *kosmos*, meaning the world or the universe. Here there is a sharp contrast with Aristotle and his belief in the inherent superiority of the Greeks. For Stoics, all human beings, equally, are sparks that emanate from the great Fire that is the being of God himself. As a result, although explicit doctrines of what we now call "human rights" (irrespective of race, colour and, later on, gender) did not appear until much later (arguably not until the 17th century CE), there is little doubt that Stoic philosophy helped to pave the way for these doctrines.

4. Neoplatonism

The tradition that came to be known as Neoplatonism (a kind of new interpretation of what was claimed to be the essence of Plato's philosophy) had many roots, but the most significant was the life and teaching of Plotinus (c. 204-269 CE). Once again, the fundamental metaphysical teaching is integrally related to the ethical teaching. In stark opposition to the materialism of both Epicureans and Stoics, Plotinus taught that the true nature of fundamental reality is what we would call mental or spiritual – corresponding to the Greek word *nous*, which can roughly be translated as mind. (We have already come across this term in the chapter on Aristotle.) *Nous* refers to *both* the fundamental reality that lies behind the universe, which Plotinus refers to as "God", and to the *core* of every human being. Nevertheless, despite the strong disagreement with Stoic materialism, there is a similarity to Stoic ethics, for in both cases good persons

---

[3] Even great philosophers are not always consistent. One commentator (W.A. Oldfather, in the 1925 introduction to his translations) suggests that in his writings Epictetus expressed a blend of monotheism, pantheism and polytheism.

must seek to purify themselves so that they can seek unity with the ultimate Godhead – conceived as the ultimate Fire by the Stoics and the absolute One by the Neoplatonists.

Part of the explanation for this combination of agreement and disagreement can be found in critical thinking concerning the word *materialism*, which has two very different meanings. The first refers to a metaphysical claim – namely, that ultimate reality is composed of matter or atoms, or some such *substance*. The second is an ethical claim – namely, that the object of the good life should be the accumulation of material things, or sheer pleasure. In English, if we say that someone is a "materialist" we may be claiming either (or sometimes both) of these two very different things. Hence we can see that in regard to the first sense of the term (concerning the metaphysical claim), Stoics and Neoplatonists are in sharp disagreement. Ultimate reality for Stoics is materialistic, but for Neoplatonists it is Idealistic (in a Platonic sense). However, in respect of the second, or ethical sense (the rejection of selfish ambition), they are in strong agreement. For both traditions, personal *purification* is demanded, and this is partly a matter of observing the traditional virtues (such as temperance and courage), but also of cultivating, both by life-style and serious meditation, the inner life of the spiritual side to our beings. Further, in both cases, while there is a strong belief in the immortality of the soul (an immortality that is the reward of the moral life), because of the potential to be *united* with the ultimate Fire (for Stoics) or the One (for Neoplatonists), it is difficult to say how far this is the immortality of the individual person that is you or me. Frequently, I suspect, both Stoic and Neoplatonic teaching on this matter was misunderstood by less informed followers, so that talk of immortality was taken (wrongly) to mean a continuation of the present individual, with its memories and passions, as well as a "centre of consciousness". As before, the use of critical thinking should lead us to ask not so much: "Is there immortality?" as "What kind of immortality is being suggested?"

In its day, Neoplatonism formed a kind of rival to Christianity, despite the fact that the two traditions had many similarities. Christians had a more individualistic interpretation of eternal life, but – more profoundly – the God of Plotinus is analogous, rather than identical, to the Christian concept of God. Perhaps the clearest difference between their different accounts of God is this: instead of the Christian (and Jewish) doctrine of *creation*, in which, by a purely *voluntary* act, God chooses to create a universe,[4] the Neoplatonists held that the physical universe is a kind of "overflowing" or "emanation" from the One absolute Mind. There is not only a certain necessity to this overflowing (in contrast with the voluntariness of creation), there is also not the radical separation between the Creator and the world that we find in Judaism and Christianity (and later, in Islam).[5]

There is little doubt that despite these differences, Neoplatonism had a profound influence on many Christian thinkers, who – although disagreeing with certain doctrines or emphases – saw similarities in the search for unity with a God that could only be achieved by moral and spiritual living. In particular, the practice of meditation, designed to reveal or enhance our relationship with God, linked the

---

[4] Plato's "maker-God", the *demiurge*, made the world or universe from pre-existing material, whereas Jewish and Christian doctrine taught that the world was made from nothing (Latin, *ex nihilo*).

[5] The Neoplatonic notion of the universe as a kind of "overflowing" of "God" or "the One" is, of course, a metaphor, and hence one can envisage ways in which the Christian (creationist) view and Neoplatonic (overflowing) view might be reconcilable, especially when one tries to interpret the idea of creation "out of nothing". For example, does "nothing" mean the same as "no thing"?

two together. Hence many Christian writers both quoted and wrote respectfully of their Neoplatonic rivals – in contrast with the polemic that characterized a lot of early inter-faith discussion. Furthermore, the practical ethics of Neoplatonists and Christians were almost identical.

5. Philosophy and Religion

We must be careful not to confuse religion with philosophy. As we have seen, philosophy, especially in the Western tradition, is a mixture of critical thinking and a set of seminal texts that illustrate this thinking. The definition of religion is more disputable, but I suggest two complementary accounts of how we should describe its nature. The first account, which will feature in later chapters, is that religions typically result from a human response to the non-rational – where we distinguish the non-rational both from the rational and from the irrational. The rational is characterized by an intellectual inquiry that is seen in the search for evidence and consistency; the irrational is characterized both by prejudice and by the deliberate ignoring of evidence and consistency. The non-rational, in contrast, is not like either of these, but refers to certain kinds of "raw experience" – such as falling in love, or being overwhelmed by natural beauty or a musical experience, or the mystical experience of sensing that one is in absolute union with the universe or with God. Only when we *reflect* on how to *interpret* such experiences do questions of rationality or irrationality enter the picture. For example, the widespread appearance of what is called *mystical* or *unitive* experience is a kind of psychological fact – something that occurs as a kind of raw experience in many cultures. In itself it is non-rational. Rationality enters when we seek to interpret what these experiences mean; for example, are they (as theists usually believe), intimations of the reality of a God, or are they perfectly well explained in terms of a secular philosophy (perhaps as the result of low oxygen levels in the blood)?[6]

The second, and complementary account of religion goes like this: "Religions are traditional ways of life in which groups of people are bound together by shared values, shared ritual activities, and things which they hold to be sacred". In other words, religions are not only individual responses to the non-rational, they also have a communal aspect. Although, for some people, religion is a purely private matter, more typically, religions reflect communal responses to the non-rational. Here, I should stress that not all philosophers will agree with me on this way of describing how we should use the word "religion".[7]

The term "sacred" refers to things that are "set apart", that is to say, given a special status, and this can relate to (i) sacred persons who are given a preeminent status (such as Confucius or the Buddha or Christ or a series of prophets); (ii) sacred *writings* (such as

---

[6] Critical thinking should help us mark an important distinction here – one that is between *conviction* (which, I suggest, may often be warranted) and an absolute intellectual *certainty* (which, I suggest, is often an example of irrationality). If a secular writer holds the conviction that mystical experience can be explained *naturalistically* (that is in terms of conventional science), say by low oxygen levels in the blood, this is one thing; if they assert that an explanation along these lines, *must* be correct, this – I suggest – indicates an irrational certainty in the truth of a position on which equally intelligent and well-informed people can disagree. The interesting issues here are further complicated by the fact that some of those who describe mystical experiences, such as Arthur Koestler, also supported atheism. Further still, if it should be proved that mystical experiences are associated with (say) low oxygen levels, this still leaves issues of causation open.

[7] Part of my argument for this usage goes as follows: if we take courses in a university department of "religious studies" we would not be surprised to find them dealing *both* with theistic religions such as Christianity and Islam, *and* religions, such as (Theravada) Buddhism, in which personal relationship to deity/ies is irrelevant to liberation. This is precisely because of the ways in which both kinds of "religion" bind communities together in matters such as ways of life and communal rituals.

the *Analects* of Confucius or the Christian gospels or the Hindu *Upanishads*); or (iii) sacred *places* (such as Jerusalem or Mecca or the temples found in many religions). If this is the best way to use the word "religion", it follows that religion is more a matter of having a set of typical characteristics than being defined by a single feature that must always apply – and this understanding of how many words function is a feature of the philosophy of Wittgenstein. It follows that sometimes there is no sharp line between a traditional way of life that clearly falls under the heading of a religion, and a tradition that does not – like certain forms of Communism. In the classical communism of the Soviet era there were features that could be called sacred: people, such as Marx and Lenin; writings, such as the *Communist Manifesto*; and places, such as the tomb of Marx in Highgate Cemetery, London. But (at least in typical cases), there were no organized rituals. Because of this lack of ritual I would tend not to class this form of communism as a religion, but the example shows how "fuzzy" the term can be. Other examples can be found in many forms of religion practised in indigenous or tribal communities, where – typically – there are no *written* sacred texts. I would still wish to class most of these as religions because (a) there may be oral traditions that serve similar functions to written texts, and (b) because of the systematic way in which these ways of life involve rituals. It also follows that although belief in a God is a typical characteristic of Western religions, it is not a typical characteristic that applies to all religions, some of which have no space for a "God" of any kind, and some of which use the term "God" in very different ways.

One clear consequence of our emphasis on critical thinking is that whenever people ask questions about *God*, we should begin by clarifying in what sense the term is being used, rather than rush straight into an argument for or against belief.

In the rest of this chapter and the following, we shall be looking at the impact of Christianity on Western moral philosophy and in the light of the foregoing, we must be careful not to see Christianity itself as a philosophy – it is rather a way of life, rooted in the desire to follow the example of Jesus of Nazareth.[8] However, many reflective Christians developed philosophies that they held to be compatible with their religion, and we shall be examining some of these in the rest of this chapter and in the next. Christianity is not unique in this: some pious Jews, such as Philo, developed Jewish philosophies; some Hindus, such as Shankara, developed Hindu philosophies; some followers of Confucius, such as Zhu Xi, developed Confucian philosophies; and so on. Notwithstanding the significant difference between philosophy and religion, there is at least one factor that links them together. This is the human response to wonder, or to what Aristotle called *thaumazein*, which he believed to be the real source of philosophy. Wonder is more than a kind of intellectual puzzlement, although it may include this; it is a kind of fascination, partly intellectual, partly emotional, that arises when human beings are confronted with aspects of reality that intrigue them. Here both the intellectual activity of philosophy, and the search for a meaning to life that characterizes religion, have a common source.

---

[8] The first Christian creed, probably used until around 80 CE, was simply "Christ is Lord" (the two words, *Christos kurios* in Greek). Trinitarian creeds came later. In other words the heart of the new faith was following the "way" of Jesus rather than believing a body of teachings.

6. Origen

Origen (c. 185–254 CE) spent most of his life in Alexandria, one of the most intellectually fertile cities of the ancient world. A Christian with a brilliant mind, he was one of the foremost *apologists* for Christianity, arguing not only for its spiritual appeal (as do all those who seek to spread a religion), but equally its *rational* appeal. The word *apology* comes from a Greek word that means a "defence", and in this context this means a *rational* defence. One aspect of this defence – the one that is particularly important for the theme of this book – is his theory of how sacred writings, in this case the Christian Bible, had to be *interpreted*. Origen argued for a threefold system, namely that with all religious texts, one has to distinguish the literal, the moral and the spiritual meaning that lie behind the words.

From the perspective of moral philosophy, this is a matter of huge importance, because if we take the literal meaning of many sacred texts there are often conflicts with ordinary ideas of morality. It was for precisely this reason that Socrates rejected many of the stories about the Greek gods, given the immoral way in which the gods appeared to behave. Correspondingly, there are many challenging passages in the books of the *Old Testament*. For example, in the book known as *Joshua*, the God of the Jews appears to command the massacre of women and children following battles at the cities of Jericho and Ai.[9] Some conservative Jews and Christians simply say: "if God commanded it, then it must be good" – but this is a response that most reflective Jews and Christians are likely to reject, among other reasons because it becomes unclear what it means to say "God is good" in any ordinary sense of the

---

[9] The massacre of the male warriors may also be problematic, especially after the battle, but at least this would be in accordance with ancient custom.

term.[10] The last 200 years has seen the rise of what is known as biblical criticism in which the Bible is subjected to the same kind of historical and literary analysis as other books. Because of this, many contemporary apologists would simply say: "This is what the ancient text says, but it does not reflect what actually happened, only what the writer *thought* happened, or *thought* that God commanded." Therefore, modern followers of religion have to select which passages they regard as spiritually important. This is a response that many apologists make now, but it would be unrealistic to think that this defence could easily have been made in the third century CE, given the kind of respect accorded to religious texts. The alternative, adopted by Origen, was to say that we must place the moral or spiritual teaching of the passage *above* the literal, even if this means, or in cases like the battles of Jericho and Ai, *demands*, that we reject the literal interpretation[11]. In effect, such passages become like parables or myths, where there is a truth to be learned from the passage, but it is not one that comes from a literal reading. Thus Origen, in commenting on this passage, says that what is really to be learned from these stories in *Joshua* is the demand to crush the vices

---

[10] The view that "good" literally means "what God wills" is known as *voluntarism* (from the Latin *voluntas*, meaning "will"). Most mainstream Christians have rejected this theory (although it exists in different forms, some of which are more subtle, and point to a kind of divine ordering of the structure of the universe, in which "good" emerges, rather than a simple identity of "good" with God's will). The more general view is that we learn our moral terms, in the first instance, from our social lives, and then discover that God is good. Without such a claim, it is hard to give significance to the claim "God is good".

[11] I am not suggesting that this is how we should *now* interpret such passages. I would argue rather that we see them as reflecting ancient beliefs that we have grown out of. Many ancient texts combine a mixture of genuine insight with outdated points of view. However, as indicated, I don't think this was a realistic option for Origen, given his times, and in consequence, I suggest that his way of stressing the moral or spiritual meaning was the best way to preserve respect for an ancient text with belief in the moral goodness of God. (Origen's suggestions can be found in his *Homilies on Joshua*.)

that are in our hearts. These are the real enemies.[12] More generally, he argues that when it comes to the interpretation of Scripture, we *must* interpret it in a way that is worthy of God. It is hard to think of a clearer example of how, for Christian apologists like Origen, Christianity was a blend of Jewish religion and Platonic philosophy. The Creator God of the Jewish tradition was also the ultimate moral Good (and the ultimate Mind behind the universe), and necessarily so. If the creator God is also the Good (e.g. of Plato), then it is essential that we interpret some texts along these lines.

7. Augustine of Hippo

Augustine (354-430 CE) was a convert to Christianity who ended his life as bishop of Hippo in North Africa. Here I want only to stress two aspects of his thought that influenced Western moral philosophy. The first is his overriding emphasis on love (*agape*) as reflecting both the essential character of God and the kind of response that God wants to draw from human beings. As in the teaching of Jesus, although rules and regulations have their place in the moral life, they ought to be secondary to the overriding demand to love our neighbours as ourselves, even if sometimes this means breaking some of the traditional rules.[13]

This emphasis on *agape* has led to a teaching on God's grace (meaning the free and enabling gift of God) that has had a major influence not only on the history of Christianity, but also on moral philosophy, because of the way it impacts on free will and moral

---

[12] He writes: "you ought to know that those things that are read [about the destruction after the battle of Ai] are indeed worthy of the utterance of the Holy Spirit". *Homilies*, chapter 8. On interpreting the Bible in a way that is worthy of God, see also Origen's *First Principles*, Book 4 (p. 287 in the translation by G.W. Butterworth).

[13] There are passages in St. Paul's Letters, especially in *Romans*, which say something like this, and it is interesting to note that Augustine was converted to Christianity while reading this same text.

choice. Augustine had a principal opponent, a British monk called Pelagius (c. 354-420 CE), and a simplified version of the controversy goes like this: Pelagius taught that human beings are free to choose between good or evil, and when we choose good, God will reward us; Augustine taught that because of human sin and weakness, none of us is able to make this choice for the good without God's grace, rather we depend on the love of God who forgives us and redeems us as we are, and not as we ought to be. It is God's election or *predestination* that secures our redemption.

Critical thinking should make us hesitant to accept the dispute in quite these terms, especially when we find that almost all of Pelagius's writings have only survived within selected quotations from his enemies. On the one hand, it is not certain that Pelagius did reject all need of divine grace; he may well have claimed that we need it to encourage or assist us in a genuine choice of the good. After all, when our friends assist us to choose well, we don't immediately say that we had no free will. On the other hand, some of Augustine's comments on the power of divine grace seem to leave little if any place for human free will, although Augustine himself claimed to uphold it. An emphasis on a love of God that reaches out to us and draws us, and for which we owe huge thankfulness, is one thing – and in this almost all Christians draw inspiration from Augustine – but explicit doctrines of predestination leave many Christians (and others) worried, because they seem to be in tension with any adequate account of human responsibility. This is one of many topics that I seek to draw attention to rather than answer, but it will be revisited in the discussion of omnipotence and omniscience in Aquinas in chapter 6.

The second aspect is Augustine's teaching concerning what is termed the "just war", a teaching that has had a profound importance in Western thought and practice, and still raises interesting ethical questions. Most early Christians were pacifists, meaning not only that they sought peace on earth, but that – more specifically – they would not take up arms to fight in any war. There were two reasons for this. First, most Christians took Jesus' command not to resist the enemy, but to "turn the other cheek" (Matthew 5.39) literally. Second, in practice, serving as a soldier in the Roman army almost certainly involved rituals in which one had to offer incense to Caesar, as a kind of god, and this was held to be too close to an idolatry forbidden to Jews and Christians. However, by the time of Augustine things had changed. After Constantine's conversion around 312 CE,[14] the Roman state gradually became more and more a kind of "Christendom" – in which Christian ideals impacted on the law and operation of the empire.

This interlocking of religion and politics is a hugely controversial matter, as it has been for Islam.[15] Many religious people think that all political states should be essentially secular (leaving religion to the private spheres of individuals or families), and independent of religion. This "secularism" – it is argued – follows from a saying of Jesus: "Render unto Caesar the things that are Caesar's and to God the things that are God's" (Mark 12.17). According to this view, the development of a political Christendom was a mistake, with bad consequences for both church and state.

---

[14] How much this conversion reflected a genuine change of heart, and how much it was a matter of political convenience, is a matter of much dispute.

[15] In the case of Christianity, the religion was a persecuted minority for its first 200-300 years, so from the start there was a clear distinction between moral law, civil law (i.e. the law of the Roman state) and religious law; in Islam, the early history was very different. From the beginning, given their military successes, Islamic cultures intermingled moral, civil and religious law. In recent times this has led to many difficulties, especially for the development of secular states in regions where Islam is paramount.

Others disagree, holding that such an intermingling of state and religion can bring a new and fruitful set of moral values to the state.

Augustine was one of a growing number of Christians who, while critical of many traditional Roman practices (such as the gladiatorial shows in the amphitheatre), felt that the Empire was also a source of peace, in which the average citizen could live and flourish. Many referred to the *pax Romana* (the Latin for "the Roman peace") to mark a period of several hundred years in which, for most of the time, trade and travel and literature flourished. In this context, Augustine disagreed with the radical pacifism of most early Christians and supported what came to be known as the doctrine of the just war, according to which, provided that (i) the cause was just, (ii) the intent was for a greater peace, and (iii) the war was "public" – meaning sanctioned by the ruling powers – then it could be just, and Christians should be prepared to fight. In particular, fighting to preserve the Roman Empire against the barbarian hordes that sought to overthrow it could be justified.

Reflection on the relationship of war to questions of justice did not begin with Augustine, although it was his view that held most sway in the Middle Ages of Europe. For example, around 400 BCE the Chinese sage Mozi taught that only purely defensive wars could be justified and – showing great personal courage – he travelled around China seeking to persuade warlords only to become involved in such wars. Later, in Europe, philosophers such as Aquinas added to Augustine's three criteria for a just war, suggesting the need for (iv) just conduct within the war, (v) proportionality,[16] (vi) last resort and (vii) some chance of success.

---

[16] According to this principle, even if a war could be justified by both cause and conduct, if the result were likely to be overwhelmingly terrible (as in a nuclear winter), it would be better not to engage in it.

Two readings from Origen's *On First Principles*, Book 4 (220s CE)[17]

One must therefore portray the meaning of the sacred writings in a threefold way upon one's soul, so that the simple man may be edified by what we may call the flesh of the scriptures, this name being given to the obvious interpretation; while the man who has made some progress may be edified by its soul, as it were; and the one who is perfect and like those mentioned in the apostle: "We speak wisdom among the perfect; yet a wisdom not of this world, nor of the rulers of this world, which are coming to nought: but we speak God's wisdom in a mystery ...(IV.2.4)

...I have no doubt that the careful reader will be uncertain in very many cases whether this or that story is to be regarded as literally true, or true in a less degree, and whether this or that precept is to be literally observed or not. Much effort and toil must therefore be exercised, so that each reader may in all reverence become aware that he is dealing with words that are divine and not human, inserted in the holy books.

Two readings from Augustine's *Against Faustus* (c. 400) [18]

What is the evil in war? Is it the death of some who will soon die in any case, that others may live in peaceful subjection? This is mere cowardly dislike, not any religious feeling. The real evils in war are love of violence, revengeful cruelty, fierce and implacable enmity, wild resistance, and the lust for power and such like; and it is generally to punish these things, when force is required to inflict the

---

[17] From the translation by G.W. Butterworth (1936) in *Origen: On First Principles* (London: SPCK, 1936).

[18] Both are taken from Rev. Richard Stothert Trans, *Against Faustus: Early Church Fathers: Nicene and Post-Nicene Fathers*, Series 1, Vol. 4, available in many places online.

punishment, that in obedience to God or some lawful authority, good men undertake wars, when they find themselves in such a position as regards the conduct of human affairs, that good conduct requires the act, or to make others act in this way. (Book 22, Chapter 74)

A great deal depends on the causes for which men undertake wars, and on the authority they have for doing so; for the natural order which seeks the peace of mankind, ordains that the monarch should have the power of undertaking war if he thinks it advisable, and the soldiers should perform their military duties in behalf of the peace and safety of the community...Since, therefore, a righteous man, serving it may be under an ungodly king, may do the duty belonging to his position in the State in fighting by the order of his sovereign, – for in some cases it is plainly the will of God that he should fight, and in others, where this is not so plain, it may be an unrighteous command on the part of the king, while the soldier is innocent, because his position makes obedience a duty ...(Book 22, Chapter 75)

Vitoria's *De Indis*

Most writers on the theory of the just war have thought their side was in the right and the other in the wrong. However, there have been some notable exceptions, where brave men and women have argued that the war their own country was fighting was wrong, either altogether, or that it was wrong in so far as it had resorted to wrongful means. An example of the former would be most of those who opposed the war in Vietnam (1955-1975), and examples of the latter are those who objected to the carpet bombing of German civilian populations in 1944, and the dropping of atomic bombs on civilian targets (Hiroshima and Nagasaki) in 1945. In both cases, though, they accepted the general need for the war. Historically, the most famous example of a philosopher arguing that his own country was waging war unjustly was the Spanish philosopher/theologian Francisco de Vitoria (1492-1546), who attacked the way in which his fellow-countrymen (the *conquistadores*) were waging war in South America. In lectures delivered in 1532 he argued that although the Spanish could reasonably use force if they were prevented from embarking on missionary enterprises or trade, the manner of the force they were using was completely unjustified. The indigenous people had a perfectly good title to their lands and culture, and this was in no way vitiated by alleged heresy or evil. He remarks, perhaps with a sense of humour or irony, that if wrongful or unnatural practices could rightfully bar leaders from the right to rule "there would be daily changes of kingdoms" in Europe!

While credit must be given to Vitoria for criticizing his own king and country (with attendant risks to himself), he was also a man of his time, some of whose views we are unlikely to share. Consider, for example, his patronizing remark about the stupidity of the indigenous people. Also, it is clear that while he thought that Spaniards had every right to preach their faith in foreign lands, the same right did not apply to advocates of other religions. His justification for this (to us) unequal treatment, is almost certainly related to his interpretation of divine law – a category of law that we shall find in Aquinas, in the next chapter.

Two passages from his *De Indis (Concerning the Indians)*[19]

It is, however, to be noted that the natives being timid by nature and in other ways dull and stupid, however much the Spaniards

---

[19] The translation used is that of John Pawly Bate from *De Indis et De Jure Belli Relectiones* in *The Classics of International Law*, ed. James Brown Scott (Washington: Carnegie Institution, 1917).

may desire to remove their fears and reassure them with regard to peaceful dealings with each other, they may very excusably continue to be afraid at the sight of men strange in garb and armed and much more powerful than themselves. And therefore, if, under the influence of these fears, they unite their efforts to drive out the Spaniards or even to slay them, the Spaniards might, indeed defend themselves but within the limits of permissible self protection, and it would not be right for them to enforce against the natives any of the other rights of war (as, for instance, after winning the victory and obtaining safely, to slay them or despoil them of their good or seize their cities), because on our hypothesis the natives are innocent and are justified in feeling afraid. (pp. 152-3)

I personally have no doubt that the Spaniards were bound to employ force and arms in order to continue their work there, but I fear measures were adopted in excess of what is allowed by human and divine law. (p. 158)

Question 1

In the light of Stoic teaching concerning the truly virtuous person, do we think that a perfectly good person should be invulnerable to inner turmoil?

Comment

Is a state of inner invulnerability compatible with the kind of "love" we should seek to promote in our children?

Question 2

Should the modern state always be completely independent of any official religion?

Comments

1. There can be ideological constraints in states even if (officially) there is no state "religion". Perhaps some such ideologies raise similar issues as the power of a particular religion, if a state is to be genuinely "secular".

2. Some states can be nominally secular (e.g. Turkey and Israel) while, in practice, a particular religion holds significant political power or privilege.

Question 3

Can we really distinguish "just" and "unjust" wars given the complexity of the modern world?

Comment

Do nuclear weapons make a difference to the way the issues should be assessed? (For example, does the possibility of a "nuclear winter" following an atomic war mean that we need to rethink the case for pacifism?)

Question 4

Should private soldiers simply obey their political rulers on the issue of whether it is right to fight in a war, or do they too have some responsibility concerning the justice of a conflict?

Comment

Pope Pius XII declared that – provided they lived in a democratic state – individual soldiers should obey their political rulers on the issue of the justice of war. Others (such as the 17th century Puritan preacher Richard Baxter) argued that at least in extreme cases, individual soldiers also carry responsibilities. He might well have argued that the U.S. "draft dodgers" (who refused to fight in the Vietnam War) were acting rightly.

Chapter 6. Thomas Aquinas and natural law

Background

In 1273, a few months before his death, it appears that Thomas Aquinas had a mystical experience of such power that, compared to the reality he had now witnessed, his writings seemed like straw. This reaction to experience, or to what I have suggested (in chapter 5) should be classed as the non-rational, makes for an interesting contrast with the strong rational emphasis displayed throughout his work. For example, he was frequently accused by more conservative Catholics of placing too high a value on reason rather than on faith. This was especially in view of his repeated claim that while theology might sometimes point to truths that go *beyond* reason, it should never support an alleged truth that was *against* reason.

The writings of Thomas Aquinas (c. 1224-1274) mark what may be called the high tide of Christian philosophy in the Western world. This is in part because of their comprehensiveness and erudition, and in part because Aquinas' views became the standard by which theological orthodoxy was often measured, at least in Western Christianity. What is known as "Eastern Christianity" or the *Orthodox* tradition,[1] has some important differences, and the influence of Aquinas is less evident. One of these differences will feature later in this chapter. Also, instead of the Catholic Pope, centred in Rome, the heads of the Eastern churches (on earth)[2] have been alternative Popes, or Patriarchs, including those resident in Athens, Moscow and Alexandria. In the next three sections I propose to outline three features of Aquinas' philosophy that influenced moral philosophy and where, as so often, we see the influence of metaphysics on ethics. What may look like a theory of causality – that might seem not to belong in a book on moral philosophy – is intimately linked to ethics.

1. Primary and secondary causality

All mainstream Christians claim not only that there is a God who is the creator of the universe and everything in it, but also that this God was active in the history of the Jewish people – a history described in the historical books of the *Old Testament*. However, despite this shared belief, different Christians have regarded the *manner* of God's relationship to the world in very different ways. According to all theistic versions of religion, God, as creator, is the ultimate cause of all things. In the view of many Christian writers, for example, John Calvin (writing some 300 years after Aquinas but expressing a much more ancient belief in an overarching

---

[1] When the lower case is used for the letter "o", as in "orthodox", this is a reference to the more *traditional* teaching of a Christian church; when the upper case is used, as in "Orthodox", this is a reference to the Eastern churches, in contrast with the Western churches – which, in turn, are often separated into the Catholic and Protestant streams of Western Christianity. The Orthodox tradition separated from the Western Catholic tradition in various stages (sometimes based on doctrinal differences, sometimes on more political ones), the chief of which is called the Great Schism of 1054.

[2] According to all Christians, the "head" of the church is Jesus Christ, but there is also, for many branches, a *human* "head on earth".

omnipotence), God is the *direct* cause of every event, including what we would now call neurological events within the human brain.[3] When a theologian wants to magnify God as much as possible, we can understand how this view of divine causation came about, because – by attributing every event to God's absolute and sovereign will – *we might seem* to be giving God all the glory that we can. Not so, say other theologians, because if God *directly* controls all events, where is there room for free will? Perhaps, still more crucially, these dissenting theologians suggest that views like those of Calvin make God responsible for all the evil and suffering in the world. For this reason we find in these same dissenting theologians a very different, and I suggest, more subtle account of God's activity in the world. According to their view – as one famous theologian wrote: "God makes the world make itself".[4] To put this in another way, instead of – as it were – pulling billions of strings in order to make things happen, God stands back from *direct* control. The situation is analogous to that of good parents who, instead of directing exactly what their children will do, stand back – at least most of the time, and especially as the children get older – and allow the children to make mistakes, even sometimes painful mistakes, because this is necessary if the children are to develop as persons.

Does this show a lack of absolute power? Here, once again, some critical thinking is helpful. What we mean by "absolute power" is ambiguous. Is it the power that one can *enforce* a whole series of *events*, or is the power designed to bring about a certain kind of *character*, as in Aristotle's account of genuine virtue? Here, as we saw in chapter 4, the person has to take part in the development

---

[3] Calvin, *Institutes of the Christian Religion* (1536) (Philadelphia: Presbyterian Board of Christian Education, 1936), 3. 22. 8; 1. 16. 8-9; 2. 3. 13; 3. 21. 5; 3. 22. 1-6.

[4] Austin Farrer, *A Science of God?* (London: Geoffrey Bles, 1981) p. 90.

of their character in order to make genuine virtue (*hexis*); that is, an acquired disposition. Becoming a person, for Aristotle, involves a *process* in which the individual plays an active part. Persons are quite unlike robots, whose actions can be totally determined by their makers.

In Aquinas we find a careful exposition of this second approach, one that depends on the distinction between (i) God as "first cause", meaning creator of the whole *system* of nature and (ii) what might be called local or secondary causes at work within the natural order (Aquinas calls them *proximate*). These exhibit their own, internal causal mechanisms. The secondary causes have a certain kind of independence from the divine will, although they do flow, ultimately, from God, because he created the whole system in which the secondary laws hold sway. Suppose that a tree falls down in a storm. If we ask *why* it fell, it is unhelpful to say: "Because God willed it to fall". According to Aquinas we should say something like: "Because the wind was too strong, given its shallow roots" (or something along those lines). Moreover – and here we come to the heart of the matter – there is a sense in which God *must* act in this way, at least most of the time (that is, if he intends to create human beings with real character and virtue), because otherwise we do not have a universe in which there can be human responsibility and love.[5] God created the system or order of nature (as "first cause"), but then allows it to run itself.

Without the kind of view suggested by Aquinas, it is hard to see how we could avoid saying that God is responsible for suffering. It

---

[5] Some Christians argue that miracles, if they ever occur, are exceptions to this general rule. Other Christians believe that such violations of the natural order never occur, and that what we call miracles refer to situations where hitherto unknown or unrecognized natural forces have come into play.

is also hard to see how the empirical sciences could have developed, for these depend on the examination of secondary causes and the laws which describe them, in which the whole universe exhibits an extraordinary and beautiful order. This universal order, in turn, provides the setting for Aquinas' theory of the natural (moral) law, as we shall see in section 3.

2. Omnipotence and omniscience

A similar conclusion emerges when we use critical thinking to ask what religious people mean when they talk of God's *omnipotence*. Some think that this means the power to do literally anything, and in response, during the European Middle Ages, some theologians asked: "Could God make a stone that was too heavy for Him to lift?" If he could, then he was not omnipotent, because having made this stone he couldn't lift it. If he couldn't make the stone, then – because he couldn't make it – again he was also not omnipotent! The proper conclusion from this example is that the word "omnipotent" is ambiguous. Aquinas was among those who were particularly sensitive to the difficulties of describing the nature of God's power. He dislikes any language which suggests that God is limited or that he cannot do certain things, preferring instead to claim that it is more appropriate (Latin, *convenientius*) to say that *it makes no sense* to speak of God either being able to break the law of non-contradiction (in other words of doing things that are strictly illogical) or being able to do what is evil (because this would be in conflict with his loving nature).[6] In less guarded language, we could say that – in the view of Aquinas – God's power is not such that he can do, literally, anything, and that this is one of many instances of

---

[6] See Aquinas, *Summa Theologiae* 1a, Q 25, As 3-4 and 1a 2ae, Q 93. A 4.

where people tend to misunderstand what a philosopher is saying.

It may be helpful to note that when people say that something is "impossible", there are at least three different kinds of impossibility that might be involved. There is:

(i) *logical* and/or mathematical impossibility (as when someone asserts that 2 plus 2 equals 5, or that they have drawn a square circle);

(ii) *practical* impossibility (as when a human being claims to have run a mile in two minutes, under standard earthly conditions); and – more controversially

(iii) what is sometimes called *nomological* impossibility (as when someone claims to have travelled faster than light). This third category refers to laws of nature (in the physical rather than the moral sense of laws) that describe how the universe works.

Aquinas' claim refers to the first, and possibly the third kind of impossibility.[7]

The meaning of *omniscience* (or "all knowing") raises similar ambiguities. Calvin argued that God knows all details of the future because he so *determines* it. Aquinas disagrees with this view, arguing that God knows the future, not for this reason, but because (following the Neoplatonists) he stands outside time and so sees all things from an eternal standpoint. This would be rather like human readers who – while reading a novel that is full of suspense – know the conclusion because they have looked at the last page. Others again – more radically – argue that in choosing to make a universe

---

[7] One of the interesting issues that arise is this: nomological impossibility might – at first sight – seem to be different from the analysis of meaning, and therefore from logical impossibility. However, some philosophers hold that certain physical *constants* (such as the speed of light) are absolutely required for the existence of any possible universe. If this is so, nomological impossibility is not very different from logical impossibility. Others hold that very different universes are possible, including some with variable speeds of light.

in which there are free human beings, God has – at the same time – chosen to limit his capacity to know all the details of the future.[8] Clearly, the extent to which any God can be held to be the *cause* of wars and sufferings depends on which of these views one takes.

3. Natural law and Aquinas' system of laws

In the last chapter (note 16) we saw that in Islam, from early times, natural law, civil law, and divine law were intertwined. Although in Christendom these three categories of law also became intertwined (because of the way in which the political powers adopted the Christian religion), Aquinas makes important *distinctions* between them. These distinctions, he claims, ultimately rest on what he calls "the Eternal law of God". This last statement is a way of saying that all kinds of law ultimately depend on a rational harmony that underlies both the inner workings of the divine mind and of the creation that is its product.

(i) Let us begin with Aquinas' category of natural law. A confusion can arise because sometimes we use this term to refer to the laws of nature in a scientific sense – thinking of the laws that describe, and up to a point perhaps, explain, how the physical world works. "Natural law" (Latin *lex naturalis*) in the moral sense is quite different and forms an integral part of most Christian accounts of moral philosophy. Natural, in this sense, is the moral law that applies to all human beings as human beings, and not as Christians, Jews, Confucians, etc. It is very similar to Aristotle's idea of universal justice which, as we saw in chapter 4, is not universal in the sense that it is universally *found*, but in the sense that it is what is universally *needed* if human beings are to flourish. St. Paul, in his

---

[8] An example of such a view can be found in the writings of the Christian philosopher Charles Hartshorne.

letter to the Romans, claimed that all human beings have this law "written in their hearts" (*Romans* 2.15) – which we might interpret as meaning "can be seen by reflection to be needed for human flourishing in society". Although there are clear differences between the details of what is held to be moral law in different societies, there is a case for seeing some foundational similarities – precisely because of the requirements for human survival and flourishing. We shall return to this theme in the last chapter, especially in the discussion of the English philosopher H.L.A. Hart. Hence it is not surprising to find versions of the Golden Rule in many religions and also in many secular accounts of morality. The Golden Rule can be found in both its positive form, namely: "Do unto others as you would have them do to you", for example in Judaism and Christianity, and in its negative form: "Do not do to others what you would not have them do to you", for example, in Confucianism.

Although most philosophers who use the term "natural law" think of it as flowing indirectly from God, there can be secular versions in which essentially the same idea of a universal moral law for all human beings is upheld, whether or not there is a God. In the 17th century, the Dutch philosopher and jurist, known as Grotius, although a Christian,[9] argued that the natural law existed for all human beings, whether or not God existed.

(ii) Civil law, which Aquinas calls "human law" (Latin, *lex humana*) is the law according to which judges, appointed by the

---

[9] Hugo Grotius, the Latinized name of Huig de Groot (1583-1645), was a devout Christian and a supporter of the Arminian (liberal) version of Calvinism. The possibility of a secular natural law was especially important for him, because as a lawyer, he was attempting to establish a viable international law that would be acceptable to all nations and peoples, regardless of their religion (or lack of). According to Grotius, the primary content of international law was provided by treaties (which he called a variety of "volitional" law), but when he came to argue for what ought to be included in these treaties he used his secular account of natural law.

state, pass judgments and award punishments. It is virtually the same as "civil law" (Latin, *ius civile*) in Roman law. There is clearly an overlap with moral law, especially when some rule is necessary for the flourishing of a civil society – and here, we return to a theme briefly discussed in the first chapter. For example, refraining from robbery is *both* a moral and natural law (because it is wrong to take other people's property without due cause) and a civil law, because it is part of the legal code of every country and its violation is punished by the state. Sometimes the two kinds of law (moral and civil) are different; for example, most people think that it is wrong, and against the moral law, to be unkind to one's grandmother and not to visit her when she is lonely. However, few of us think that the civil law ought to enforce this moral rule. Here (in the rule that one ought to be nice to one's grandmother) we have a moral but not a civil law. Further, in some political regimes there can also be a clash between the two types of law. For example, in Nazi Germany, the civil law demanded that you betray Jews living in your neighbourhood, so that they could be taken away to concentration camps and killed; most of us would think that the moral law tells us to protect these same people. Aquinas argued that, in a sense, this human law is derived from natural law, because although the details of civil law depend on particular decisions of the legislature, the general rules are required by natural law, because it is the moral duty of the state to promote the common good. For example, natural law dictates that a sovereign should forbid robbery, but whether the penalty should be prison or some other sanction, and how long a prison term should be, are matters for political judgment. The way in which moral and civil law are related can also be seen from how we distinguish between countries governed by the "rule of law" and countries torn apart by strife, where we might say "the rule of law has broken down". This requirement for a working civil or human law, in order for people to flourish, helps to explain Aquinas' claims about how human law "flows" from natural law and how, at least most of the time, it is a requirement of natural law that we obey the human or civil law.

(iii) The term "divine law" is ambiguous. Sometimes religious people simply use it as another term for natural law, because they hold that God commands all people to be moral; however, in a strict or narrower sense, it is distinct from natural or moral law. When Aquinas writes of divine law in the strict or "positive" sense (Latin, *lex divina*), he is not referring to natural law, but rather to obligations we have solely because we are Jews, or Christians, or Muslims, etc. The ritual law of the *Old Testament* is one example; a demand on Christians to attend church another; the demand that Muslims fast in the month of Ramadan another. None of these is required by a universal morality. The idea can be clarified by imagining the situation when we are on board a ship. As passengers, we are obliged – as at all times – both by (i) natural law, or general moral obligations (e.g. not to be rude to fellow passengers) and (ii) by the local civil law (e.g. not to rob fellow passengers); but also we are specially obliged, beyond these matters (iii) to obey the captain when there is an emergency. When the captain commands: "Take to the lifeboats", we have an additional kind of obligation, one that we tacitly accepted as soon as we came on board, namely to accept the authority of the captain when there is an emergency. Similarly, positive divine law puts special obligations on groups of people who hold that they have some kind of covenant with God – one that parallels a kind of "covenant" we make when we board a ship.

I want to end this section by stressing again how Aquinas' view of natural law – the universal morality that applies to all people – flows from his more general philosophy of secondary causality.

We have seen that, according to Aquinas, all created things, such as trees, flourish or fail to flourish, according to the secondary laws that describe the natural workings of the whole system of nature. However, human beings have – as it were – a double stake in this secondary, semi-independent world. First, like everything else, their physical bodies flourish or fail to flourish according to natural causes. Also – as we shall note in the first reading from Aquinas' *Summa Theologiae* – we can actually *participate* in the divine plan, because when we seek to *reason out* what makes for the common good, we are actually *participating* in the divine ordering of the world. This is an interesting idea, and perhaps reflects the Stoic and Neoplatonic belief that our intellects, in a sense, can participate in the Mind of God.

4. Some problems

Aquinas' moral philosophy has many positive features and helps to make sense of how some people can combine an understanding of how morality applies to all human beings, regardless of their particular religion or lack of religion, and at the same time, how we can appreciate the influence and significance of a particular religion, even if we do not ourselves share any of the beliefs. Also, we can appreciate the good and bad points of a religion, whether or not we participate in it. Here, it might be helpful to contrast three different approaches to how religion and ethics – in general – are related. First, there are those who think that religion is necessary for morality. This faces the obvious problem that there seem to be many highly moral people who have no religion.[10] Second, there are some who think

---

[10] While the claim that religion is essential if people are to be moral seems refuted by this observation, a more subtle claim, namely that religion is needed for holding a moral philosophy that is adequate for grounding human rights, is more defendable. Philosophers disagree about this claim.

that religion is basically bad for morality, stressing, for example, its tendency to persecute those regarded as heretics. This, I suggest, is an over-reaction that ignores the praiseworthy moral endeavours of some religious people, who have been driven, at least in part, by their religion. Consider, for example, the Buddhists who attacked the caste system and the Christians who attacked slavery. Third – and I suggest much more realistically – we see how religion, while separate from morality, can also influence it *either* for evil or for good. The history of persecution illustrates the potential for evil; the history of the abolition of slavery illustrates the potential for good.

Referring to negative aspects of religion, I want to indicate three problems that occur in the Catholic theology that Aquinas advocated, all of which are important for moral philosophy.

(i) Most Catholic philosophers, including Aquinas, have held that human beings are born not only in original sin (which, as we shall see, can mean different things), but also with an original "guilt" (Latin, *culpa*).[11] This belief is based, in large measure, on a highly misleading translation of a passage in St. Paul (*Romans* 5.12). Where the original Greek text suggests that we all sin in the manner of Adam, the early Latin translation read "we all sin *in Adam*". In contrast, the Greek Orthodox churches (which, of course, fully understand the original Greek text) have always interpreted what Christians call "original sin" to mean not "original guilt" but something like "original moral weakness". This avoids the claim that babies are born with any inherent *guilt*, claiming instead that forgiveness is only needed once human beings co-operate with evil. Guilt can only apply when our wrongdoing (or what Christians call

---

[11] This issue was raised in note 7 of chapter 4.

"sin") has been voluntary.[12] This means, among other things, that when babies are baptized in the Christian churches, there is no guilt to wash away (as with adults); it is rather that they are entering a community where sin can in the future be removed. In chapter 11 when we consider the philosophy of Marxism, I shall argue that when original sin is taken to mean a human condition of moral weakness (and not guilt), both for individuals and societies, there is much to be said for it. The economic conditions may help to drag humans into misbehaviour, but they are not the sole cause. Typical human beings face an internal moral struggle between their more noble instincts (such as love of our children) and less noble ones (such as a lust for power). Again, we may recall Plato's powerful image of the human soul as that of a charioteer trying to control two very different horses.

(ii) I have already referred to the intolerance often shown by many religions, and the persecutions that have often followed. Interestingly, atheism, when combined with any kind of ideology, can be just as intolerant and persecutory – as witnessed by Stalin's reign of terror. Aquinas, despite his many virtues, saw no inherent problem in the persecution of those deemed heretics, and in 1252, during his lifetime, we find a decree (*Ad extirpanda*) that formally approved the torture of heretics (although with certain reservations, such as the protection of life and limb).[13] Sadly, when the Protestant movements emerged in the 1500s, many of them proved just as intolerant as the Catholics, although there have been some notable

---

[12] Some Catholic philosophers, such as Abelard (1079-1142 CE), also made this claim, but they were then in danger of being declared heretics.

[13] Part of the explanation for this acceptance of intolerance was the belief that if you died holding false theological opinions, this might cause your punishment in the next life. In what are often termed "liberal" versions of Christianity, this is denied, unless the false views are the result of deliberately-chosen ignorance. For example, the Anglican writer, William Chillingworth (writing in 1638) wrote that the only absolute moral demand was to endeavour to do the good, as we saw it.

exceptions, as amongst the Quakers.

(iii) Until recent decades, traditional Christianity, in all its forms, has held highly questionable views both on the status of women and on sexual ethics. In maintaining the superiority of the male, they were following one of the less worthy aspects of Aristotle's philosophy, but they also relied on certain Biblical claims, taken literally, such as the claim that the husband is the head of the family.[14] Equally troubling has been a frequent insistence that the chief purpose of sexual union is simply procreation, so that any sexual act in which this is prevented is wrong. In recent decades many Christians have interpreted their holy writings differently. The total equality of men and women is now insisted upon in all the churches that are called liberal, and furthermore, sexual acts that help to build or cement loving relationships are generally deemed good, even if there is no possibility of producing children. Unfortunately, the official position of some churches (even though often ignored by many followers), still declares that any use of artificial birth control is intrinsically wrong – a famous example being the Catholic teaching enshrined in the papal encyclical of 1968, *Humanae vitae*.[15] In view of the huge problem of world overpopulation, this is a cause of disquiet.

Readings from Aquinas' *Summa Theologiae* (1265-1274)[16]

From 1. 2ae, Question 92, Article 2.

Now among all others, the rational creature [a human being]

---

[14] E.g. *I Corinthians* 11, 3.

[15] This encyclical (a kind of official letter sent to all the churches) also bans the sterilization of men or women, even if they have had many children. It does, however, allow what is called the "rhythm" method of birth control (which attempts to limit sexual activity to the parts of the menstrual cycle in which the woman is unlikely to conceive).

[16] Adapted from the English Dominican Fathers: *The "Summa Theologica" of St. Thomas Aquinas*. London. Burns and Washbourne, 1911-1938.

is subject to Divine Providence in the most excellent way, in so far as it partakes of a share of providence, by being provident both for itself and for others. Wherefore it has a share of the Eternal Reason, whereby it has a natural inclination to its proper act and end: and this participation of the Eternal Law in the rational creature is called the natural law.

Comment

As indicated, here we see an explicit claim that because of their capacity for reason, human beings can actually participate, knowingly, in the divine plan. In addition to echoes of Stoic and Neoplatonic thought, this can be understood as a footnote to Plato's claim that the enlightened soul, that has come to be able to look at the sun (representing the Idea of the Good), can begin to share in the understanding of ultimate reality.

From 1. 2ae, Question 96, Article 2.

Wherefore human laws do not forbid all vices, from which the virtuous abstain, but only the more grievous vices, from which it is possible for the majority to abstain; and chiefly those that are to the hurt of others, without the prohibition of which human society could not be maintained: thus human law prohibits murder, theft and such like.

Comment

Here we can see clearly (i) the role of human law in promoting the common good, and (ii) the way in which the natural (moral) law demands virtues that go beyond the requirements of civil or human law.

From 1. 2ae, Question 96, Article 4.

[Human] laws may be unjust in two ways: first by being contrary to human good ... either in respect to the end, as when an authority imposes on his subjects burdensome laws, conducive, not to the common good, but rather to his own cupidity or vainglory - or in respect to the author, as when a man makes a law that goes beyond the power committed to him - or in respect to the form, as when burdens are imposed unequally upon the community, although with a view to the common good. The like are acts of violence rather than laws; because as Augustine says... "a law that is not just seems to be no law at all". Wherefore such laws do not bind in conscience, except perhaps in order to avoid scandal or disturbance, for which cause a man should even yield his right ...

Comment

This is one of the passages that has led some commentators to refer to Aquinas as a kind of liberal (or even a radical socialist), because if taken literally this text suggests that all kinds of tyrannical laws do not bind in conscience and should be resisted. However, in practice, Aquinas rarely approved of civil disobedience, still less of open rebellion, and his safeguard "except perhaps in order to avoid scandal or disturbance" may help to explain this.

Question 1

Is Aquinas right to believe that there is a universal moral law that applies to all human beings, regardless of their race, religion and gender? How do we account for the differences between what different cultures approve and disapprove in matters of behaviour?

Comment

Perhaps contemporary claims concerning universal human rights amount to a secular version of the natural law?

Question 2

Is human nastiness the product of human nature, the environment, individual perversity (or all or none of the above)?

Comment

Was Marx right to claim that given the right environment both law and state could "wither away" (because – so Marx claimed – it is basically the wrong environment that leads to "alienation" and not any "original sin")?

Chapter 7. Hobbes and the impact of materialism

Background

Although Thomas Hobbes was not the first philosopher to discuss contract theories of political government (even Plato considered versions of it, for example, in his dialogue, the *Crito*) Hobbes is probably the first major figure to make the notion central to his theory of politics. A key question in moral philosophy is this. If we have a general moral obligation to obey the law of the state, is this because in some way we have *agreed* to do so (either explicitly or implicitly, through some kind of contract); or does our obligation arise from other considerations, such as our duty to support the common good?

When we come to the philosophy of the Englishman, Thomas Hobbes (1588-1679), we find that we have moved into a very different world from the European Middle Ages. Although the philosophy of Aquinas continued to have influence in Catholic countries such as Italy and Spain, Europe had begun to move into what is sometimes called the "modern" era. The causes of this change included the following factors:

(i) The Protestant Reformation, starting around 1517, reduced the power of the Catholic Church and tended to boost the role of the individual – in part because of the claim that ordinary people, not just the clergy, should be free to read and to interpret the Christian Bible.

This claim also reduced the power and authority of the clergy.

(ii) This increased power of the individual, especially of educated males, was facilitated by the growing economic prosperity of many towns and cities. Instead of a medieval divide between landowners, clergy and peasants – with relatively few people in the professional and artisan classes – we now have large urban populations of artisans and professional people of many kinds. This totally changed the dynamics of social and political life.

(iii) Modern states, with relatively powerful central governments, had replaced medieval feudalism in which local lords held almost absolute power. One reason for this was an increasing use of cannons, which – unlike the unreliable ones of the Middle Ages – could reduce a feudal castle to ruins within a few days. This gave the ruling monarch much more control of the whole country.

(iv) The Renaissance – starting in Italy in the 14th and 15th centuries – had spread throughout Europe, reintroducing the study of ancient classics and encouraging new ways of thinking, in part because educated people became aware of the questions asked by the likes of Plato and Aristotle.

(v) Printing with moveable type was increasingly making books available to more and more people. Printing with woodblocks had been invented in China long before, certainly by the eighth century CE, but the first whole book printed in Europe was in 1455.

(vi) The empirical sciences (as we have seen, championed by Aristotle but not pursued by most of his followers), were beginning to transform the way in which philosophers explained our knowledge of the world.

Taken together, these six factors help to explain the very different world in which Hobbes wrote.

1. Hobbes and physical materialism

In chapter 5 we noted that the word "materialism" has two very different meanings: first, a philosophy of ultimate reality, claiming that either atoms, or some other "substance", is the ultimate reality out of which everything else is made; second, a moral philosophy that claims that material goods, leading to happiness or pleasure, are the proper goal of human life. The Stoics, for example, were materialists in the first sense only. Hobbes, by contrast, was a materialist in both senses.

Let us begin with the first sense. Here Hobbes is of major importance, because the most common objection to physical materialism – at least in our age – is that the "stuff" out of which everything is said to be made seems to become less and less solid with each new scientific discovery. We are discovering that atoms are made up of subatomic particles and that these particles seem to be much more like fields of energy, or mathematical formulae, than anything we could think of as a "substance". Although Hobbes lived long before discoveries concerning subatomic particles, he took a step which transformed materialistic philosophy and made it much more coherent and tenable for the modern world. Essentially, instead of "stuff" or "substances", he redefined materialism in terms of laws of motion. In taking this step he was hugely influenced by the work of Galileo, among others, and his discovery of planetary motion. In consequence, the main body of Hobbes' writings was conceived as applying the laws of motion in three domains. First, in his *De Corpore* (Latin for *Concerning Bodies*), he would give his account of the physical universe and the laws of motion that govern it. Second, in his *De Homine* (Latin for *Concerning Mankind*), he would give his account of the laws of motion that govern and explain both human behaviour and human motivation. Third, in his *De Cive*

(Latin for *Concerning the Citizen*), he would apply the same laws of motion to political philosophy. In practice, for a mixture of political and personal reasons, the three projects did not appear in the order originally planned, and all three were later incorporated into his most famous work, the *Leviathan* (1651). All three projects were intimately related, however, and show once again how it is impossible to draw a sharp line between moral philosophy and more general issues, such as those of metaphysics and the philosophy of science.

There is a further complication. In Hobbes' method we do not find a straightforward example of what later became standard scientific method, because Hobbes' method was rather an interesting and complex blend of mathematical reasoning and empirical studies, an account of which would take us beyond the scope of this book. However, it is worth recalling that this entwining of mathematics and the empirical sciences is a bequest from the ancient Greek philosophers and their fascination with mathematical reasoning, which was later, in the case of Aristotle, combined with empiricism.

I will close this section with a note regarding Hobbes' religion which has implications for his moral philosophy. Materialism is frequently associated with atheism, and many of Hobbes' contemporaries certainly regarded him as an atheist. In part, this is because he insisted that any talk of terms such "immaterial substances" is – like talk of "square circles" – simply meaningless. Here, in his rejection of traditional metaphysics as literally meaningless – as the 20th century logical positivists argued – Hobbes can be seen as a precursor of some 20th century philosophers. However, for three reasons, just labelling Hobbes an atheist is to oversimplify the situation. First, he denied that he was an atheist.

Second, in some of his correspondence,[1] he seems to have held that God did have some kind of (very ethereal) body. Third, in denying any rational discussion of the nature of God, Hobbes can be interpreted as allying himself with those religious writers who stress God's ineffability. The existence of God is not necessarily denied, only any rational knowledge of his nature.

2. Hobbes, ethical materialism and free will

The implications of Hobbes' philosophy of motion for ethics are dramatic. He insists that all interior thought is simply a matter of interior motions of *appetite* (when we are drawn to some object of desire) or *aversion* (when we are repelled by some kind of pain). The mental processes we think of as reasoning are chains of such interior motions, and our decisions are simply the last acts in this chain. Here we have a classic example of what philosophers call *reductionism*. All inner thought processes can be *reduced* to tiny, *physical* movements within the brain. In the case of deliberation (which is a relatively organized sequence of such interior motions) he writes: "In Deliberation, the last appetite, or Aversion, immediately adhering to the action, or to the omission thereof, is that we call the Will."[2] The claim, by many contemporary scientists and philosophers, that all aspects of self-consciousness can be "reduced" to accounts of neurological activity within the brain, can be seen as a modern version of this. For Hobbes' philosophy, two consequences of major importance for ethics follow:

(i) The first is an absolute insistence that all motives for action are purely selfish and driven by our appetites for personal goods

---

[1] Correspondence with Descartes and Bishop Bramhall.
[2] *Leviathan*, chapter 6.

of some kind. It is not simply that our personal drives happen to be egoistic, *they could not be otherwise*. Later, this account of personal motivation (which is both a philosophical and a psychological claim) came to be called *psychological hedonism*. The view that we *ought* to pursue our own long-term interests is found in a number of philosophers, from some Sophists to the present day, and sometimes goes under the heading of *enlightened self-interest*. Self-interest in this view is a kind of supreme moral principle. However, it is important to see that Hobbes is saying more than this. It is not simply that we *ought* to pursue our own long-term self-interest, it is that we *cannot* think or act otherwise. Later in this chapter I shall argue that on this matter Hobbes' position cannot possibly be correct.

(ii) The second consequence is an account of what is meant by free will that is still accepted by some philosophers. Hobbes claims to believe in human freedom, but only in the sense that the source of free action is within us (rather than being constrained by outside forces). Effectively, he identifies "free" actions with what Aristotle called "voluntary" actions. In chapter 4, we noted that Aristotle did not discuss the contemporary problem of free will[3] – he was concerned with the general issue of when we could be considered liable for what we do. In our own day, even this useful distinction, when applied to legal responsibility, needs to be modified by factors such as the "insanity defence". Hobbes insists that we have "freedom" whenever our bodies are not controlled by outside forces (either literally, when we are picked up and moved, or in a more

---

[3] In the ancient world there was discussion of free will, but almost always in the context of how we could combine human freedom with divine Providence. The contemporary debate centres on the very different issue of how – if at all – we can combine our growing knowledge of the scientific laws that govern neurological activity with any account of inner freedom. Hobbes' discussion is one of the first to see the issue in this way.

subtle sense, when a burglar points a gun at us). But any suggestion that we are "free" in some other sense, as, for example, Aquinas held, was to talk nonsense. Hobbes' reduction of mental states to physical movements made any such suggestion incoherent. This raises an issue that is still very much alive and I shall depart from the historical flow of this chapter to discuss it briefly.

Although it is often those from a religious background who emphasize human free will, they are frequently joined by many purely secular philosophers. Both groups take the position that an over-arching determinism[4] should be challenged, and that there are grounds for believing that human beings have a faculty that can be called "free will". The situation is further complicated – as indicated in chapter 6 – by the fact that some religious writers, especially in the tradition of John Calvin[5], do not give any space for what most people mean by free will (even when they claim otherwise), because of the way in which God is believed to determine the inner activities of the brain. In defence of free will, one line of argument goes like this. The secular philosopher J.S. Mill (who features in chapter 9) argued that certain properties "emerge", for example, during the course of evolution, and that although we might be able to trace the steps by which these new properties emerge, once present,

---

[4] I am not suggesting that reductionism is always a mistake; on the contrary, it can be part of a valuable analysis that tends to break things down into smaller components. By the term "overarching reductionism", I refer to what is a questionable *assumption*, namely that there are virtually no limits to how far this reduction can go.

[5] Jean or John Calvin (1509-1564) was a French theologian who founded one of the Reformed traditions of Protestantism, which includes denominations such as Scottish Presbyterianism. Doctrines include the rejection of much post-biblical tradition, the self-government of church congregations, and the assertion of predestination.

they require a new and more subtle kind of analysis.[6] In particular the language we use to describe this new property cannot simply be "reduced" to language that does not take account of the new property. When we attempt to do so, something is – as it were – "lost in translation". The most obvious example is the emergence of biological life from what is sometimes called the primeval sludge of

---

[6] The passages appear in his *System of Logic*. Mill himself did not go on to link this argument with a defence of "free will" – which he thought was an unnecessary metaphysical complication.

An important discussion of emergent properties occurs in John R. Searle's *The Rediscovery of Mind* (Cambridge, Mass: MIT Press, 1992), pp. 111ff. Searle endorses *part* of what I am claiming, a position that he calls "emergent1", namely that "consciousness cannot itself be deduced or calculated from the sheer physical structure of the neurons without some additional account of the causal relations between them". Thus he rejects a "nothing but" version of reductionism that identifies mind and brain as just two ways of talking about the same thing. However, he does not endorse my suggestions about what I would like to call a "transcendent" quality of the developed human consciousness, similar to what he refers to as "emergent2", according to which "consciousness could cause things that could not be explained by the causal behavior of the neurons" (p. 112). Even if it is the case that human thought is always mirrored by an accompanying neurological activity, I am not convinced about the universal causal priority of the latter. Further, behind all the argumentation there are often fundamental world-views that either support or question an overarching "scientific naturalism" or "physicalism". Both terms refer to the theory (or belief) that absolutely all things can, in principle, be fully explained in terms of contemporary, scientific methodology, including the very existence of the universe.

The issues are often clouded by the assumption that the alternative to an overarching physicalism is a return to Descartes' dualism in which there is an absolute divide between the world of things (technically, "extension") and of thoughts or minds. More likely – I suggest – is a third option, in which the complementarity of the physical and the mental is explored.

"This notion of complementarity has become an essential part of the way physicists think about nature and Bohr has often suggested that it might be a useful concept also outside the field of physics." Fritjof Capra, *The Tao of Physics* (3rd ed. London: Harper Collins, 1993), p. 173.

On the theme of overarching physicalism, see also Thomas Nagel's *Mind and Cosmos* (Oxford: Oxford University Press, 2012), where the subtitle reads: *Why the Materialist Neo-Darwinian Conception of Nature Is Almost Certainly False*. Nagel, it should be stressed, writes from a strongly secular point of view.

amino acids and such like, hundreds of millions of years ago. The point should recall Aristotle's account of the "organisms" (one step in his Great Chain of Being) that make up the vegetable level of being. Their nature is such that the inter-relationship of their parts is intrinsic or *constitutive* of what they are. It is not that they are necessarily more complicated than a strange pile, say, of stones or crystals, but that they are complicated in a different way. Although Mill himself did not take this next step, supporters of free will can argue that a similar step-change occurs once we have self-conscious life. We should note that such a claim does not have to include any suggestion that this new, emergent property, is unique to human beings, or that it comes – as it were – suddenly; it could emerge gradually, perhaps with something equivalent to flashes of insight.

Consider, for example, the recognition or insight that a particular mathematical argument is valid, or that a particular empirical argument is sound. If this recognition can be reduced to a neurological description of certain movements within the brain, how do we know that this description marks real insight? Perhaps, the insight is marked by another higher order set of neurological activities? But how do we know that this set is really a higher order one? We find that once we deny some genuine, intellectual ability to *recognize* a valid or sound argument (in a sense of recognition that is essentially different from any account of a neurological pattern), it is hard to avoid an infinite regress, with each level of neurological activity facing the question: "How do we know that this pattern represents what is a truly valid or sound argument?" My suggestion is that – in addition to the emergence of biological life – there is another kind of emergent property that comes with self-consciousness, a property that we label "free will", and that at this level words like recognition and insight become coherent, and indeed necessary. It is perfectly natural that we cannot explain this new level simply in the language of material motions, as reductionism assumes. It can, however, be described within the framework of the "interior" language that we find – among many other places – in good literature, such as novels and poetry, and in what philosophers call *phenomenology*.[7]

3. The state of nature, and civil government

The most famous of all Hobbes' claims relate to what he called "the state of nature". This is defined as a situation in which there is no political sovereign ruling over us, so that – given the egoism that Hobbes believes drives all of us – we live in constant fear and dread. We fear not only natural disasters (of the kind that civil society partly protects us from) but, more worryingly, other people, who – as they seek their own benefit – might reasonably think they can protect themselves by harming us. Hobbes did not necessarily think that this state of nature referred to an actual historical situation – more likely it is a kind of myth that describes what human life would be like without civil government. The Jewish and Christian story of the Garden of Eden, inhabited by Adam and Eve, is another example of a story concerning human origins that almost certainly was not intended to be history.[8] Hobbes concludes his description of the state of nature in these famous words: "No arts, no letters, no society, and what is worst of all, continual fear and danger of violent death:

---

[7] Defences of the truth and/or coherence of free will should not depend on references to the indeterminism of modern physics. If there is a faculty properly referred to as free will it is neither purely deterministic, nor based on the randomness that goes with the indeterminism of subatomic particles.

[8] In this case the Biblical author or authors give a clue, because the word "Adam" in Hebrew has three overlapping meanings: a proper name, a word for "mankind", and – in a slightly different form – the "earth" from which Adam was made.

and the life of man, solitary, poor, nasty, brutish, and short."[9]

Faced with this reality – rooted in the analysis of human nature – what is the rational person to do? Hobbes' answer is clear, and in the context, perfectly understandable. The rational, egoistic person seeks a way out of this situation, and realizes that the only way out is for everyone to *submit* to an order in which they behave differently because they fear the sovereign power more than they fear each other. A "law of nature", in Hobbes' use of the term, is a general rule, found out by reason "by which a man is forbidden to do that which is destructive of his life, or taketh away the means of preserving the same, and omit that by which he thinketh it may be best preserved."[10] A series of rational considerations follow – according to Hobbes – the most crucial being the following:

First, in order to make for peace (which is necessary for our well-being) all must be willing to lay down their own natural right to do whatever they will (in order to protect themselves) *provided that others do so too*. Second, Hobbes argues that from this it follows that having made a *covenant* or (what we might now call a contract) with others, we *ought* to keep this covenant – because it is only this covenant that can assure all of us that we have security. The covenant, by necessity, sets up a sovereign government, which we rationally fear because of its power to punish – and we rationally fear this sovereign more than we fear our fellow citizens.

4. Some criticisms and problems

This short summary of Hobbes' position cannot do justice to the brilliance of the language, and – in a sense – a kind of remorseless

---

[9] *Leviathan*, chapter 3. In this and the other quotations from *Leviathan*, I have modernized the spelling and punctuation.

[10] *Leviathan*, chapter 14.

logic that follows *if* one accepts the premises on which the argument is based. Sometimes there is also considerable wit, as when he likens politics to the game of cards, but with the proviso that in politics "clubs are always trumps".[11] Moreover, there is this to be said in favour of Hobbes' overall argument: in times of crisis, over and over again, most people will prefer an autocratic government to the kind of chaos that arises when there is political disorder or civil war. Further, this preference for autocracy rather than chaos is perfectly rational, if we are to preserve our lives. Nevertheless, there are some major problems with Hobbes' overall argument, and I shall indicate three of them.

(i) Psychological hedonism. The theory of psychological hedonism is untenable in the light of animal studies that show that the inner drive of many animals, including human beings, is not simply for self-preservation, but for that of the gene pool. Indeed, the development of this "unselfish" drive is necessary for evolution. Parent birds will frequently sacrifice their lives to protect their young from predators, and even human beings sometimes choose to give their lives for their friends. The desperate counter-argument that such persons *must* be motivated purely by the selfish thought of rewards in heaven is simply absurd – even if it is true in some individual cases. One way of describing ethical dilemmas is to say that human beings (and perhaps other animals) are frequently faced with two competing internal drives, both required by evolution – one to protect ourselves, the other to protect our gene-pool – and that one source of ethical dilemma is our quest to balance these competing desires. I do not think that this is the whole story, especially when rational reflection

---

[11] A typical English pun, based on two meanings of "clubs", one a kind of card used in games, the other a weapon – and of course, for Hobbes, the political sovereign carries all the relevant weapons.

enters the scene, but it is an interesting way of describing how ethical problems can arise.

However, this rejection of psychological hedonism does not totally destroy Hobbes' overall argument; it only requires that it should be put more carefully, and structured in terms of everyone's ardent drive to protect either themselves, or – at the least – their nearest and dearest. In other words, a similar logic can be constructed that expands our psychological drives to include the protection of those close to us, especially our families.

(ii) The free rider problem. Hobbes believes that by use of his argument he has shown how we can derive a genuine *moral* obligation from a purely *prudential* one. A prudential argument shows how we *ought* to do x, *if* we want to achieve y (and, as we shall see in chapter 10, this is not what we normally think of as a *moral* "ought"). In contrast, a moral argument shows that we *ought* to do x, because it is the right thing to do, not just because we want to achieve y. Hobbes needs to make this move from prudential to moral obligation if he is to show that having made a covenant, we *ought* to keep it, even if we think that we might get away with breaking it. The "free rider" is someone who outwardly goes along with the covenant, and says that he will obey even when the police aren't watching, but will not obey if and when he thinks it is in his private interest not to obey and that he can escape punishment. Hobbes is clearly aware of this crucial problem for his overall philosophy and makes a gallant attempt to cover it, by – as I put the matter – attempting to derive a genuine moral ought from a prudential ought, by way of the promise to obey the covenant.

Hobbes' argument just doesn't work. Suppose I want to be a free-rider, and believe that I am much cleverer than most people. I would then reason as follows: I can see that in order for civil society to exist, and in order to avoid "the state of nature" most people must obey the covenant, even when there are no policemen watching, but the system will still work provided that only a very few people, including me, just pretend to go along with the system. Since – according to Hobbes – my only drives are for my self-preservation it is logical for me to "get away with it" if I can. If I add in some drives on behalf of my nearest and dearest, representing my gene-pool, a similar argument can be put forward. In short, there is no such thing in Hobbes' philosophy for a genuine *moral* obligation. However, once one person can reasonably argue along these lines, it is difficult to put a limit on how many can and will do so, and – I suggest – this indicates a failure to be able to generate any genuine sense of moral obligation from the foundations that Hobbes sets out in his materialistic philosophy. If the derivation of genuine moral obligation is necessary for the maintenance of human society, as Hobbes appears to think in his theory of covenants, then it is, in my view, fatal to the logic of the whole scheme.

Some commentators have tried to cover the gap between moral and prudential obligation in Hobbes by reference to Hobbes' notion of God as somehow providing a ground of obligation that goes beyond the purely prudential. The issue here is whether God is to be feared simply because of his power to place us in heaven or hell (a view which would conform to Hobbes' general theory of human nature), or whether – as some philosophers have suggested – he can actually command respect in a different way, one that can begin to look like genuine moral rather than purely prudential obligation.[12] I am skeptical of this latter view, but the fact that it is supported by

---

[12] See, for example, F.C. Hood, *The Divine Politics of Hobbes* (Oxford: Clarendon Press, 1964).

some intelligent commentators illustrates how difficult it is to be certain about exactly how to interpret some passages in Hobbes. It is certainly the case that in *Leviathan* he gives far more space to religious questions than might be expected. The central problem is this – so long as any God or gods are feared and obeyed because of their power, then we have not moved towards *moral* obligation, but only a longer-term prudential one. God can only be a source of *moral* obligation when (as in early Christian thinking), he is in some way identified with Plato's "Idea of the Good", whose appeal is other than that of sheer power.

(iii) The justification of absolutism. According to Hobbes, any adequate sovereign has to be absolute and undivided – commanding obedience in all matters. This includes how religious texts that are used within the state should be interpreted, and the outcome of any moral or philosophical dispute. Otherwise, Hobbes argues, discords can arise that endanger the state. In view of the religious wars that Hobbes observed, we can understand how he came to hold this view.[13] However, in many parts of the world we observe the viability of what are often called "liberal democracies" that seem to survive fairly well, without the absolute sovereignty that Hobbes seems to think is necessary. As in ancient Greece, much of the time all kinds of different religions, philosophies and life-styles can be tolerated. Further, in contrast to Hobbes' undivided sovereignty, many contemporary democracies have what is called a separation of powers, whereby the executive (the power than runs and organizes the state, day by day); the legislature (the institution that debates and enacts legislation); and the judiciary (including the crucial functions

---

[13] However, it should be stressed that Hobbes' sovereign did not always have to be a monarch – it could, for example, be some kind of democracy, provided that it was clear where sovereignty lay (say, in a Parliament), and that it was absolute and undivided.

of interpreting laws and appointing judges) are at arm's length from each other. In the U.K., for example, since at least 1610, there have been some important judicial decisions that have limited the power of either the executive or the legislature.[14] If Hobbes' philosophy were sound, it would seem that such democracies could not flourish, or perhaps even survive. It might be argued that such democracies can only emerge gradually, when there exists, for example, a substantial and well-educated middle class, while other cultures cannot have such democracies imposed (as some U.S. presidents seem to have thought), but only encouraged to "grow" (for example, by increasing education and reducing corruption). Whatever our particular point of view, it would seem that Hobbes' political philosophy does not adequately account for the existence of some relatively successful democratic societies where there is significant separation of powers. Absolutist government does not seem to be the only solution to how political power must be organized.

Readings from Hobbes' *Leviathan* (1651)[15]

[From the Introduction]

For seeing life is but a motion of limbs, the beginning whereof is

---

[14] I refer to the decision of Chief Justice Edward Coke [pronounced Cook] in Bonham's case, 1610.
The idea of the separation of powers in a healthy democracy has been of major importance in political philosophy. Two philosophers are especially associated with it, namely the English philosopher, John Locke (1632-1704) and the French philosopher Baron de Montesquieu (1689-1755). In the former's *Second Treatise on Government* (1690) Locke describes the powers as those of legislative, executive and federative. Montesquieu's *De l'esprit des lois (Spirit of the Laws*, 1748) uses the more familiar distinction between legislative, executive and judicial, and comes closer to how most later thinkers have thought of the relationships. Both have been of huge influence, for example, on the U.S. Constitution.

[15] The reading from the Introduction especially is from The Harvard Classics version (Cambridge, Mass: Harvard University Press, 1909-1914).

in some principal part within; why may we not say that all 'automata' (engines that move themselves by springs and wheels as doth a watch) have an artificial life? For what is the 'heart' but a 'spring'; and the 'nerves', but so many 'strings'; and the 'joints' but so many 'wheels', giving motion to the whole body, such as was intended by the artificer? 'Art' goes yet further, imitating that rational and most excellent work of nature, 'man'. For by art is created that great 'Leviathan' called a 'Commonwealth', or 'State' (in Latin civitas) which is but an artificial man; though of greater stature and strength than the natural, for whose protection and defence it was intended; and in which the 'sovereignty' is an artificial 'soul', as giving life and motion to the whole body; the 'magistrates' and other 'officers' of judicature and execution, artificial 'joints'; 'reward' and 'punishment,' by which fastened to the seat of sovereignty every joint and member is moved to perform his duty, are the 'nerves', that do the same in the body natural ...

[From chapter 14]

The right of nature, which writers commonly call jus naturale, is the liberty each man hath, to use his own power, as he willeth himself, for the preservation of his own nature; that is to say, of his own life; and consequently, of doing anything which, in own his judgment and reason, he shall conceive to be the aptest means thereunto.

By liberty is understood, according to the proper signification of the word, the absence of external impediments; which impediments may oft take away part of a man's power to do what he would, but cannot hinder him from using the power left to him, according as his judgement, and reason shall dictate to him...

Whensoever a man transferreth his right, or renounceth it, it is either in consideration of some right reciprocally transferred to himself, or for some other good he hopeth for thereby. For it is a voluntary act: and of the voluntary acts of every man, the object is some good to himself. And therefore there be some rights which no man can be understood by any words, or other signs, to have abandoned or transferred. At first a man cannot lay down the right of resisting them that assault him by force to take away his life, because he cannot be understood to aim thereby at any good to himself...

[From chapter 18]

...*by this institution of a Commonwealth, every particular man is author of all the sovereign doth; and consequently he that complaineth of injury from his sovereign, complaineth of that whereof he himself is author, and therefore ought not to accuse any man but himself; no nor himself of injury, because to do injury to oneself is impossible. It is true that they that have sovereign power may commit iniquity, but not injustice or injury in the proper signification.*

Question 1

Is there any room in Hobbes' philosophy for a distinction between a legitimate and an illegitimate government, other than its sheer power? Would we wish to make a distinction in some other way?

Comment

In 1660, when Charles II was restored to the English throne, Hobbes faced the problem that – according to his theory – while Oliver Cromwell held power (following the revolution that began in 1642), this power made him the legitimate sovereign. Hobbes attempted to fudge the issue by arguing that while in exile Charles still had some *de jure* right, but it is hard to see how this could be meaningful within Hobbes' philosophy.

Question 2

Hobbes suggests that the sovereign can commit iniquity, but not injustice – because essentially "injustice" is defined as breaking the contract, and the sovereign, although set up by the contract, is not himself party to it. What then can it mean when Hobbes claims that the sovereign may commit iniquity? Is he introducing a moral consideration that is not subject to the sovereign's interpretation?

Comment

Possibly there is an inconsistency here in Hobbes, but there is no inconsistency if what he means is simply that "iniquity" arises when the sovereign foolishly acts in a way that is likely to endanger his own grip on power (for example, by encouraging a successful revolt). But if this is all that Hobbes means, there would seem to be nothing "iniquitous" in a sadistic tyrant choosing to torture some of his subjects for his own pleasure, provided that this did not endanger his grip on power! This issue helps to explain why some commentators think that Hobbes' God does have a role to play – in this case, by holding a tyrant to account.

Chapter 8. Hume and the Enlightenment

Background

The eight philosophers who have been accorded chapters to themselves in this book are all examples of thinkers who have had a profound effect on moral philosophy. It is not because we ought to agree with their views, but because no understanding of Western moral philosophy could fail to take their views into account. They are, in part, constitutive of Western moral philosophy. Hume, through his emphasis on certain Enlightenment themes, and on the role of "passion", is one of these seminal thinkers.

1. The Enlightenment context for the philosophy of David Hume

Just as Hobbes can be seen as a representative of a new wave of thinkers, representing a kind of *modernism*, so David Hume (1711-1776) should be understood as a representative of the movement known as the Enlightenment, found throughout Europe in the 18th century. However, in both cases we must be careful not to forget the individual elements that made these movements significant. Let us begin with some of the features that caused Enlightenment thinkers to be classed together, despite personal and regional differences.

(i) Reason and science. We have seen that during the European Middle Ages (c. 500-1500 CE) some philosophers, including Aquinas, stressed the rational aspects of both philosophy and religion. But even they saw faith as at least equally significant, and many theologians considered reason to be a very secondary, and – particularly for the less-educated – a dangerous rival to the *faith* that people needed if they were to be assured of salvation. When Protestantism emerged just after the Middle Ages, the emphasis was often still less on rationality. Both Luther and Calvin, the two major figures of early Protestantism, believed that human reasoning powers are fatally corrupted by our sinful nature. In contrast, the Catholic tradition did not believe that human reason was so thoroughly corrupted; and some Protestant traditions shared this view and attempted to use reason as a divine gift. Most Enlightenment thinkers, however, shifted away from faith as a means to knowledge and most repudiated conventional religion. One major reason for this was what they regarded as religion's neglect or downgrading of rationality.

As in the case of Hobbes (where reason was thought to involve both mathematics and the use of empirical sciences), the Enlightenment trust in reason could be argued to be somewhat naive, but it certainly included an optimism about the power of empirical science. A major factor in this was the general acceptance of a key claim by John Locke[1], namely his rejection of "innate ideas". We are not born with any innate knowledge, Locke insists; rather, all our knowledge, other than mathematical, comes from or through experience. Strictly speaking, according to Locke, even mathematical knowledge was not innate, only our capacity for it – hence the emphasis on the empirical sciences[2].

In France a substantial group of Enlightenment thinkers were known collectively as the *philosophes*, among them, Diderot,

---

[1] John Locke (1632-1704), an important English philosopher who wrote right at the end of the 17th century.

[2] These sciences are not just the natural or "hard" sciences such as chemistry, but all those focusing on the study of external reality, such as history.

Voltaire and Condorcet. This word is simply a French translation of "philosophers", but in practice it refers to a group of philosophers *with a particular style of thinking*. In many cases these *philosophes* regarded themselves not so much as original thinkers, as disseminators of the works of scientific genius that stunned the world in the 17th century – such as Isaac Newton's writings on gravity. This enterprise was much helped by the social phenomenon of coffee houses, where, in many European cities, educated people would gather not simply to drink coffee, but to discuss the ideas and controversies that were current in the intellectual world. This is an interesting example of how a social practice can have dramatic consequences for the intellectual life of a whole society[3]. Tellingly, in the highly influential French *Encyclopédie*, edited by Denis Diderot between 1751 and 1765, the article on *philosophe* says: "Reason is to the *philosophe*, what grace is to the Christian."

(ii) Reason and progress. Many ancient thinkers saw history as essentially circular. This included the first Western historians, the Greek writers Herodotus and Thucydides. In contrast, writers in the Jewish and Christian traditions tended to see history as *directional* – because it told a *story* that included Creation, the Fall, the prophetic messages, the coming of the Messiah[4] and finally a Second Coming or "end of the world" event. On this view, history revealed a kind of divine plan and worked towards a kind of destination. However, this notion of direction did not necessarily imply "progress" as it is now commonly understood, because as the story of God's plan unfolded the lot of the common person was not necessarily better; in

---

[3] See Brian Cowan, *The Social Life of Coffee: The Emergence of the British Coffeehouse* (New Haven: Yale University Press, 2005)

[4] Jesus in the case of Christians and Sunni Muslims, another who is yet to come on the part of Jews.

fact, it might often be worse. In contrast, most Enlightenment philosophers thought that now, with the dawn of scientific rationality, a means of real progress – material, moral and cultural – was virtually guaranteed. The philosophes often saw themselves as having the equivalent to a divine mission, namely, to spread the application of rational and scientific approaches to all human problems, so that the world would become an increasingly better place for all humankind. Human history was not only directional; it was progressive.

2. Hume's epistemology and the role of passion

The Enlightenment had many regional variations, and David Hume was a key figure in the Scottish version, centred in 18th century Edinburgh. It had its own coffee houses and also a number of clubs where men met for conversation and argument. Other cities in Scotland also had an active intellectual life, and it is interesting to note that during Hume's life, while there were only two universities in England, Scotland, with a much smaller population, had five. It was a vibrant scene, and among the Edinburgh intellectuals of the same period, we find the philosopher and economist, Adam Smith, author of *The Wealth of Nations* (1776).

Hume, as a thoroughgoing empiricist, insisted that all our ideas were internal copies or reflections of "impressions" – the sense-experiences we all have when we receive messages through any of our five senses. What then of our sense of "self"? Earlier empiricists thought that knowledge of oneself was a kind of exception to the general rule, and that we had some kind of direct, non-empirical access to our inner selves, rather than being dependent on sense-experience. In response, Hume argued that we have no evidence or rational ground for believing that there is some insubstantial "self" independent of our ideas of it. Whenever we try to enter into our own inner world, looking for some evidence for the existence of this self, we find nothing other than these ideas – hence, Hume's famous account of (what we call) the self as a "theatre of perceptions", rather than an entity or soul. This did not mean that he belittled personhood; it was rather that persons are special kinds of *bodies* that we encounter through our senses, and whom we believe, like us, to have inner ideas and feelings similar to our own.

Given this thoroughgoing empiricist philosophy, how can we construct any rational account of ethics? Hume's answer is straightforward and immensely influential: ethics is not a matter of reason, but of *passion*. He writes: "Reason is, and ought only to be the slave of the passions, and can never pretend to any other office than to serve and obey them."[5] In modern English the word *passion* is often used for some particularly strong inner drive or emotion, as when we might refer to someone as "passionate". It is important to see that this is not what Hume has in mind. For him, "passion" is rather a general word for all the emotions or feelings that we have, and which – unlike thoughts by themselves – *drive* us or *draw* us in a certain direction, somewhat in the way that Hobbes referred to *appetites* and *aversions*.

Here we enter one of the great issues in Western philosophy: In what sense, if any, can reason by itself actually *move us*? Plato did not give a direct answer, but he provided a model, or parable, that indicates an awareness of the issues that arise. At the end of chapter 4 we noted his model of the human soul comprising two horses and the charioteer, who – all together – form a kind of representative of the inner self. Although this might be taken to mean that only passions (represented by the two horses) could actually cause any

---

[5] Hume, *A Treatise on Human Nature*, Book II, part III, section III.

movement, this is not quite what Plato suggests, for it seems that the charioteer has some power to effect change by the way he pulls on the reins. There is a further complication. We saw that when Plato talks about "reason" he doesn't always mean only "academic" reason – for instance, using our knowledge of causation to bring about change. Sometimes, at least, he seems to mean some kind of intuitive insight that approaches what we mean by love. It was this that makes understandable his otherwise absurd claim that no-one knowingly does evil.

Once again we find that critical thinking often involves being careful about the meaning of words. Hume uses the term "passion" for any kind of interior sense that can move us in some direction. His position is clearly very different from that of Plato, but the difference is not quite as absolute as it might seem.

3. Hume on utility and sympathy

Although both Hobbes and Hume depart from Aquinas' account of natural law – which carries a *rational* appeal of a potentially universal kind – they are poles apart on the issue of egoism. Whereas Hobbes sees all humans as being under the sway of selfish drives, the passion that Hume specially emphasizes in his moral philosophy is "sympathy" for the wellbeing of others – a sympathy that, he claims, is empirically observable in the vast majority of human beings, and which it is the proper business of education to foster. He writes that men, having now rejected old-fashioned hypotheses and systems in natural philosophy, "...should attempt a like reformation in all moral disquisitions; and reject every system of ethics, however subtle or ingenious, which is not founded on fact and observation."[6] Further,

---

[6] Hume, *An Enquiry Concerning the Principles of Morals*, section 1.

we can observe empirically that what tends to evoke passions of approval is the contemplation of things that have *utility* – that is to say, things that tend to foster the common benefit of human beings. He writes: "Usefulness is agreeable, and engages our approbation. This is a matter of fact, confirmed by daily observation. But, *useful*? For what? For somebody's interest, surely. Whose interest then? Not our own only; for our approbation frequently extends further. It must, therefore, be the interest of those who are served by the character or action approved of; and these we may conclude, however remote, are not totally indifferent to us." Shortly afterwards he adds: "Here is a principle which accounts in great part, for the origin of morality. And what need we seek for abstruse and remote systems, when there occurs one so obvious and natural?"[7]

With regard to the passion or sentiment of sympathy Hume writes: "Sympathy, we shall allow, is much fainter than our concern for ourselves, and sympathy with persons remote from us much fainter than that with persons near and contiguous; but for this very reason it is necessary for us, in our calm judgement and discourse concerning the characters of men, to neglect these differences, and render our sentiments more public and social."[8]

This claim that the passion we call sympathy not only explains how we can act properly in regard to others, but is also something that – because of its weakness – we should seek to promote by education and example, raises an interesting issue that might undermine Hume's position. Hume is *recommending* that we promote and enhance this passion, more than others – but, if we have rejected any appeal to rationality in this matter – *why* ought we to promote

---

[7] *Ibid*, section 5.
[8] *Ibid*.

this particular passion? Hume's answer, I suggest, might go like this: "I have this passion called sympathy, so it is natural that I should seek to promote it. The more it becomes a universal characteristic of human beings, the more my passion will be realized. There is no inconsistency in using reason (instrumentally) to work out the consequences that will help a passion to be fulfilled." I can see merit in this reply, but it has two interesting implications. First, when we begin to calculate the consequences of promoting something for the sake of general human happiness, we start to move in the direction of utilitarianism – and in the next chapter I shall indeed argue that Hume was one of the philosophers who set the scene for this important development. Second, how would Hume respond to someone whose major passion is not sympathy? Any suggestion that their passions are in a *wrong* order would seem to be importing some quite different (perhaps Platonic or rational) consideration into his empiricist ethics. In the quotation above Hume referred to "our calm judgements and discourse concerning the characters of men", and it can be argued that here he is, after all, introducing some rational consideration that is not easily reducible to those passions that, he claims, should rule our reasons. Any suggestion that it is a "calm judgement" that makes the fulfilment of one kind of passion intrinsically superior to the fulfilment of another, does not sit comfortably with a pure empiricist.

4. Hume's legacy: emotivism and the is/ought distinction

Since the time of Hume, what are often referred to as *emotivist* theories of ethics have abounded. Instead of reason, or Platonic intuition, or divine revelation, the clue to understanding moral philosophy – according to all emotivist theories – is the fact that human beings have passions or emotions, and so, all these theories agree, it is these emotions that generate what we think of as moral obligation or duty or our sense of what is right and wrong. Some of these theories will feature in chapter 11, when we review the complex and bewildering scene in contemporary Western philosophy as it has unfolded in the last hundred years. However, while the general term "emotivist" is used for many contemporary theories, it is important to realize they also have important differences. Also, it is more accurate to say that Hume is a source or ground for emotivist philosophers, rather than to class him as one, since the term was not widely used until the 20th century.

Many emotivist theories have as one of their starting points the fact/value or is/ought distinction that is first made explicit by Hume. Here is an influential passage from his *A Treatise of Human Nature* (Book III, part I, section 1). I have slightly modified the spelling and punctuation.

"I cannot forbear adding to these reasonings an observation, which may, perhaps, be found of some importance. In every system of morality, which I have hitherto met with, I have always remarked that the author proceeds for some time in the ordinary way of reasoning, and establishes the being of a God, or makes observations concerning human affairs, when of a sudden I am surprised to find, that instead of the usual copulation of propositions, *is*, and *is not*, I meet with no proposition that is not connected with an *ought*, or an *ought not*. This change is imperceptible; but is, however, of the last [i.e. greatest] consequence. For as this *ought*, or *ought not*, expresses some new relation or affirmation, it is necessary that it should be observed and explained; and at the same time that a reason should be given, for what seems altogether inconceivable, how this new relation can be a deduction from others, which are entirely different from it."

Philosophers have interpreted this passage in at least two

ways. In the first, Hume is not saying that you *can't* derive "ought" statements from "is" statements, but that we should note that when we do so we have essentially changed the force of what has been said, and therefore some explanation – one that justifies this change of force – is needed.

The second (and in my view more probable interpretation) is to say that, as a matter of logic, you *can't* derive *ought* statements from *is* statements. In order to see more clearly the logic of this claim, consider the case of someone who argues: "It is a fact that Napoleon was a tyrant, and therefore we *ought* not to honour him." The lesser problem with this argument is that not every historian would agree with the premise "Napoleon was a tyrant". However, the major problem arises even if all people agreed that Napoleon was a tyrant, and it is that the word "tyrant" is what can be called a loaded word; that is to say, its use already implies something morally bad, and therefore some kind of *ought not* can be derived. To put this another way, there is no illogical derivation of *ought* from *is*, in this case, because the *ought* has already been *sneaked* in once the adjective "tyrant" has been accepted.

Consider a less obvious case. Suppose an economist argues as follows: "Following the great European war of 1914-1918 there was a depression in which millions of people, especially among the poorer classes, suffered severe hardship. It therefore became imperative that the world leaders took remedial action." Here, by using a term such as "it became imperative", it is true that an *ought* has been introduced into the argument, but a supporter of Hume would likely argue as follows: "In most human contexts, certain descriptions carry a morally loaded force, because some (usually unstated) assumptions are shared. Those hearing this argument would almost certainly share the view that 'severe hardship' is a bad thing, and one that we *ought* to seek to prevent or remove". To put this in another way: if this argument were presented to an intelligent robot (that had not been trained to make value judgments from the mere fact of certain painful situations), the robot might respond: "Why is it necessary to take remedial action? Why does it matter if the poorer classes suffer?" This might seem like an absurd response, but it only seems absurd because, from childhood, most human beings have certain values and moral obligations drilled into them. Our language, especially when it concerns social relations, is rarely, if ever, value-free; so that the implications for *ought* are – as it were – hidden within the emotional overtones that accompany many words and many apparently purely descriptive statements. If this argument is sound, then Hume is essentially correct, although perhaps he should have been clearer about the hidden ways in which loaded words or descriptions explain how it can look as if we have derived *ought* from *is*.

A reading from Hume's *An Enquiry Concerning the Principles of Morals*, (1748) section III, part 1.[9]

Were there a species of creatures intermingled with men, which, though rational, were possessed of such inferior strength, both of body and mind, that they were incapable of all resistance, and could never, upon the highest provocation, make us feel the effects of their resentment; the necessary consequences, I think, is that we should be bound by the laws of humanity to give gentle usage to those creatures, but should not, properly speaking, lie under any restraint of justice with regard to them, nor could they possess any right or property, exclusive of such arbitrary lords. Our intercourse with them could not be called society, which supposes a degree of equality; but

---

[9] The text can be found online (usually reproductions of the 1777 edition) including Project Gutenberg.

absolute command on one side, and servile obedience on the other. Whatever we covet, they must instantly resign: Our permission is the only tenure, by which they hold their possessions: Our compassion and kindness is the only check, by which they curb our lawless will: And as no inconvenience ever results from the exercise of a power, so firmly established in nature, the restraints of justice and property, being totally useless, would never have place in so unequal a confederacy.

This is plainly the situation of men, with regard to animals; and how far these may be said to possess reason, I leave it to others to determine. The great superiority of civilized Europeans above barbarous Indians, tempted us to imagine ourselves on the same footing with regard to them, and made us throw off all restraints of justice, and even of humanity, in our treatment of them.

Question 1

Is it true that this passage has worrying implications for the way people with significant disabilities should be regarded?

Question 2

Does any serious account of human rights (e.g. for the severely disabled) demand an analysis of rights that cannot be reduced to the implications of human passions?

Comment

Hume clearly disapproved of the way in which European settlers treated indigenous peoples, but again, in their case, can we build an adequate account of human rights on the basis of Hume's philosophy?

Question 3

Does it make any sense to say that animals have rights, and if so, on what basis?

Comment

Interestingly, although many religions have a poor record in terms of the treatment of non-human animals (with some notable exceptions, as manifested – in the case of Christianity – in the lives of the Venerable Bede and of St. Francis of Assisi), it is arguably easier to acknowledge human duties towards animals – for their own sakes rather than ours – from some religious premises. A number of religions teach moral obligations to respect all aspects of created nature. In contrast, the implication of Hume's philosophy is that our duties to animals centre solely on how they will best fit our purposes.

Chapter 9. J.S. Mill and Utilitarianism

Background

Jeremy Bentham was not the first philosopher to think that the consequences of our actions are important for morality. However, he does appear to be the first to argue that they are the sole ground for moral evaluation, and that they should be measured by "the greatest happiness of the greatest number".

1. Some definitions

Following our emphasis on the clarification of terms – which, as we have seen, is one aspect of critical thinking – I shall begin this chapter with some definitions. In the context of moral philosophy, *consequentialism* refers to a philosophy in which what is right or wrong is totally dependent on the consequences of how we act. This is in contrast with *deontology*, which refers to a moral philosophy in which what is right or wrong depends on the principle or principles on which the action is taken. To take an example, consequentialists would say that lying is wrong – at least most of the time – because and only because the consequences of lying are bad. A deontologist would say that lying is wrong because there is a moral principle – "Lying is wrong" – and this principle is not simply referring to the consequences, but to some rule.[1] Whether or not lying is wrong in all circumstances is an issue that will be taken up in the next chapter.

Utilitarianism is a version of consequentialism, one in which the relevant consequences are measured by *utility*. *Utility*, in turn, has been given different meanings (although they all refer in some way to what is useful). What is called "classical utilitarianism" – which is the utilitarianism propounded by Bentham and Mill, despite some disagreements between them that we shall come to — is a particular version in which the measure of utility is the greatest happiness principle, that is to say "the greatest happiness of the greatest number". This chapter is concerned with classical utilitarianism.

2. Jeremy Bentham's utilitarianism

The English philosopher and legal theorist, Jeremy Bentham (1748-1832), is the leading figure in the early days of utilitarianism. He did not invent the theory; indeed it is hard to find any one founder (unlike, say, Epicureanism) because it grew rather than began. For example, we have already seen that Hume put great emphasis on utility. Utilitarianism also had links with Enlightenment thinking, because Bentham was even more anxious than Hume to make moral philosophy a branch of science. However, where – for Hume – this meant following the empirical method, for Bentham it meant – essentially – turning ethics into a *quantifiable* science. The root idea here is what is called "the hedonistic calculus". *Hedone*, as we saw in chapter 4, is the Greek word for pleasure, and Aristotle made an important distinction between this word and *eudaimonia*, meaning

---

[1] There is an interesting complication here. If the deontologist says that the rule exists because of the probable consequences, then either we might have a more complex version of consequentialism, or there might be some overlap between the two theories. What may be called "hard-line" deontology insists that the existence of a moral rule is not because of the consequences, and we shall see in chapter 10 that this is how Kant saw the matter.

"happiness" or "well-being". Bentham made no such distinction, and this was crucial for his claim that all happiness could, in principle, be quantified. Effectively, all forms of pleasure and happiness (which he identified) could be measured in units (let us call them *haps* though this was not Bentham's term). Pain, similarly, is quantifiable, in this case in negative haps. This is the basis for what is called Bentham's "hedonistic calculus".

Let us suppose that we are deciding whether or not it would be right to execute Smith, who has been convicted of murder. We begin by putting down the probable positive effects of executing Smith instead of sending him to prison for a long term – taking into account not only the number of items, but also the *degree* of pleasure or pain involved. We then list the negative effects and total up the result. The calculus might begin like this.

On the positive side:

1. The consequences for the family of the victim who (in this particular case) are, for the most part, glad about the execution, +48 haps.

2. The benefit to those who (in this case) would have been future victims following the release of the killer from prison, +34 haps.

3. The benefit to the taxpayers who do not have to fund long-term imprisonment, +71.[2]

4. All the other likely benefits, +213.

Total 366 haps.

On the negative side:

1. The psychological pain felt by the murderer prior to his death, -88 haps.

---

[2] It has been claimed that the cost of the long-term imprisonment is actually less than the cost of execution, when all the costs of the many appeals are taken into account. This is a factor that makes the financial argument for the death penalty hard to evaluate.

2. The pain caused to the murderer's family in contemplation of his death, -55 haps.

3. The pain caused by campaigners for the abolition of the death penalty, -66 haps.

4. All the other likely negative consequences, -120 haps.

Total -329.

Difference: + 37 haps. Therefore, the execution is a good thing!

Of course, this example is totally absurd for several reasons: (i) we could never be this precise about the consequences – the best we could do is make reasonable guesses; (ii) we could never be sure that we have included all the persons involved; (iii) we could never be sure what the long-term consequences might be; and so forth. Bentham would accept all of this, but he might have responded as follows: "First, I am telling you what it *means* to say that an action is (really) right or wrong – the fact that we often are not sure is another point entirely. Second, in many cases it is quite clear where the overall balance will lie, because some of the figures will easily outweigh all the others. In the case of the execution of Smith, the fact that it is difficult to be sure where the balance lies is important and relevant, because it helps to explain why this issue is so controversial. However, contrast that example with a possible attempt to justify, say, slavery. Here the negative figures, especially for the slaves themselves, will very clearly outweigh the pleasure that might be alleged on behalf of the slave owners."

Thus the hedonistic calculus is not offered as a precise way of solving all our moral problems, but as a way of understanding how they should be understood (e.g. what would count as a proper solution) and how we should *try* to solve them. In particular, the phrase "the greatest happiness of the greatest number" is not a reference to what the majority happens to want, because although – as Bentham put the matter – "everyone is to count for one"[3], when we take into account the intensity and degree of the pleasures and pains involved, then the right action is not necessarily the one that will benefit most people; it is the one that, numerically, will maximize overall happiness.

There are at least three good things to say about this approach to ethics, even if (like myself) one cannot altogether accept utilitarian philosophy. First, almost all of us would agree that the consequences of our actions are a relevant factor in deciding what is right and wrong (even if, unlike strict Utilitarians, we do not think that it is the *only* factor). At the least, this gives us a method of beginning to think, rationally, about moral dilemmas. Asking ourselves: "What are the likely consequences for everyone's happiness of the proposed course of action, or piece of legislation?" is a useful starting point, even if it is not the only question to ask. Second, Bentham and his followers – within a political and economic group known as "the philosophical radicals" – actively campaigned for improvements to British law, particularly those that would benefit the majority of people, including the poor. Some of their campaigns, for example in respect to the use of the secret ballot and the liberalization of laws allowing trade unions, had success.[4] Third, Bentham drew attention to the need to

---

[3] One can easily see how utilitarians tend to be on the left of the political divide, because the pleasures and pains of every individual worker or peasant ought to count just as much as the individual pleasures and pains of the landowner or aristocrat.

[4] The influence of the philosophical radicals declined after around 1840, in large measure because they did not attract many followers among the working classes. One reason for this was their paternalism. J.S. Mill, for example, thought that government should be for the benefit of all, and since in many countries most people were poor, this meant emphasizing their well-being. Nevertheless, government – he held – was the responsibility of the middle classes. See, A. Seth Pringle-Pattison, *The Philosophical Radicals* (London: Blackwood, 1907), pp. 28-9.

treat non-human animals in an ethical way. Whether or not animals had "rationality", there was no doubt they could suffer, and this meant that the consequences of our actions on all animals ought to be taken into account in all our decision-making. The contemporary sensitivity to the treatment of animals is partly a result of utilitarian philosophy.

3. Mill's version of utilitarianism

John Stuart Mill (1806-1873), the son of Bentham's close friend and colleague, James Mill, is by far the most famous utilitarian philosopher. As he developed as a thinker he gradually adopted his own version of utilitarianism that differed in some important ways from the position of Bentham. I shall indicate three of these differences:

(i) Psychological hedonism. Mill rejected Bentham's psychology/philosophy which insisted (in a way that echoes Hobbes) that we *can* only act in a way that we believe will lead to *our* own happiness. In Bentham, this led to suggestions about legal reform that was designed to bring into line what is good for the greatest happiness of the greatest number with what is good for us as individuals. This, he thought, could be achieved through changes in the civil law that promoted rewards and punishments, which, in turn, would lead to our actions being *both* for the common good (the greatest happiness of the greatest number) and for our own private good. Mill approved of most of Bentham's legal reforms, and thought it wise to align public and private good in this way, but not because this was the only way in which people could be persuaded to act for the common good. He was perfectly clear that sometimes (as in Hume's stress on the passion of sympathy), we can and do act for the benefit of others, whether or not this will, in some way, also be for our long-term benefit. He referred, in particular, to the existence of our "social feelings".

(ii) Types of happiness. Mill also disagreed with Bentham's claim that all forms of pleasure/happiness are on the same scale. Bentham had famously claimed: "if the quantity of pleasure be the same, pushpin [a children's game] is as good as poetry." In contrast, J.S. Mill wrote: "It is better to be a human being dissatisfied than a pig satisfied, better to be Socrates dissatisfied than a fool satisfied". As Mill's quotation suggests, the issue here should remind us of Socrates' claim that "the unexamined life is not worth living", as discussed in chapter 2, and reflects one of the abiding issues in moral philosophy. What is the purpose (if any) of human life? Is it - as "hedonists" claim - maximizing our own pleasure or happiness? Is it – as some followers of religious traditions claim – finding what God's purpose is for us in some kind of vocation? Is it – as Aristotle believed – developing the virtues that make us fully human? Is it – as humanitarians (both religious and secular) claim – improving the lot of humankind?, etc. Mill thought that it was something similar to the humanitarian ideal – but with a stress on the higher, or what he actually called the "nobler" kinds of happiness. Perhaps there is a hint of elitism here, because Mill (like Aristotle) is favouring certain aspects of human nature, notably those associated with friendship and the high arts. Mill responds to this charge, claiming that anyone who has experienced both the "lower" and "higher" forms of pleasure will be sure to favour the latter.

Although I personally agree with Mill's position on this matter, his argument suffers from circularity. Supposing that someone who has experienced both pushpin and poetry maintains that they really prefer pushpin, how would Mill respond? I suspect that Mill would simply say that they couldn't have *really* experienced poetry! As a matter of logic, I suggest that the *argument* here is unsound, even though the *conclusion* may be correct. If I am right, then it looks as if most of us are not prepared to lump all kinds of human happiness together. Suppose, for example, that the ruling powers were able to keep themselves in power by making sure that most citizens were content with an endless supply of "bread and circuses" (free food and entertainment), as in ancient Rome, but at the cost of having no freedom; the logic of Bentham's position is that, provided this maximized overall happiness, this would be all right. The logic of Mill's position is that it would not be all right, because higher forms of happiness associated with being free persons would have been sacrificed for the sake of lower or less noble ones.

Mill's insistence that some forms of pleasure or happiness are intrinsically more noble than others has a dramatic consequence with regard to the quantification of happiness. It becomes literally impossible, even in theory. Quantification demands that the numbers we add are all reducible to the same unit. In English the problem here is sometimes referred to as that of trying to add together apples and oranges – which we can only do if we introduce some other concept, such as "fruit", that covers both.[5] The consequence is that while Mill may well have made utilitarianism more acceptable and more rational by making this move to accept diffcrent forms of happiness, Bentham's aim of making it a quantifiable science has, in effect, been abandoned.

When utilitarianism is taken to refer to the kind of philosophy advocated by Mill, rather than Bentham, we can now see why some philosophers do not think that it is radically in conflict with deontology (with its emphasis on moral principles). To put this in

---

[5] Those familiar with philosophy will see that here is yet another example of problems concerning if and when some form of "reductionism" is justified.

another way: when utilitarianism is defined in a stark, Benthamite way (as a theory that only considers consequences for the greatest happiness of the greatest number, and using quantification), then there is a clear contrast with a deontology (when that too is defined in a stark way — one that says that duty, based on obedience to moral rules, is the whole story of ethics). However, as soon as we move to more subtle accounts of either philosophy, the differences are less clear, and some important commentators, such as the English philosopher Richard Hare, insist that they see no absolute contradiction.[6]

(iii) Liberty and the tyranny of the majority. J.S. Mill's most influential writing has been his essay *On Liberty* (1859).[7] Here, as he makes clear at the beginning, he is not concerned with the metaphysical issue of the freedom of the will but with the practical moral issue of political liberty which, as just suggested, he considered to be an essential aspect of the higher forms of happiness. Following a discussion of the emergence of democracy (meaning, in some sense "rule by the people",[8] in contrast with autocracy or tyranny),

---

[6] Some philosophers propose a kind of utilitarianism in which, instead of looking at what actions, taken in themselves, are most likely to maximize happiness, we should try to locate which rules, when generally followed, are most likely to maximize happiness. The question then arises: is this really a version of utilitarianism or of deontology (i.e., a rule-based ethic)?

[7] J.S. Mill's writings that express the most different views from those of Bentham, and his father, James Mill – including his positive assessment of the very different philosophy of Samuel Taylor Coleridge – all occur after the death of James Mill in 1836. There seems little doubt that the younger Mill held back from expressing some of his disagreements while his father – whom he hugely respected – was still alive.

[8] In ancient Greek the word *demos* had at least two rather different senses. It could mean "the people", and this is how supporters of "democracy" use the word, as in government "of the people, by the people, for the people" (in the words of Abraham Lincoln in his Gettysburg Address of 1863); or it can mean "the mob", and this helps to explain why some people have had hesitations about approving "democracy".

we find one of Mill's most distinctive contributions to political philosophy, the danger of "the tyranny of the majority".[9] He writes: "The will of the people, moreover, practically means the will of the most active part of the people – the majority, or those who succeed in making themselves accepted as the majority... 'the tyranny of the majority' is now generally included among the evils against which society requires us to be on its guard". In some ways, he argues, this is a greater danger than old-fashioned tyranny by (say) an ancient emperor because "it practises a social tyranny more formidable than many kinds of political oppression, since, though not usually upheld by such extreme penalties, it leaves fewer means of escape, penetrating more deeply into the details of life, and enslaving the soul itself."[10] To put this another way: if I lived in ancient Rome, even though the emperors exercised an extreme form of tyranny, provided I lived well away from Rome, most of the time I could probably get on with my life without great interference. This would be especially true if I were a relatively prosperous male citizen. In contrast, if I lived under some oppressive but popular religious regimes, or under the communist rule in East Germany after World War II, I might well be in constant dread of my fellow citizens, who would be likely to report any behaviour or language or statement of belief that infringed the established order. This would be a tyranny of a more pervasive kind.

4. Some conclusions

Both Hume and J.S. Mill have had profound effects on European

---

[9] The idea of the danger of the tyranny of the majority, within democracies, had been introduced by the French philosopher and political scientist, Alexis de Tocqueville, notably in his book *Democracy in America* in 1835.

[10] J.S. Mill *On Liberty*, introduction.

moral thought, even though on some matters they are in stark contrast. Take, for example, the is/ought, or the similar fact/value distinction, underlined by Hume – a distinction that underlies much moral philosophy, as will be evident in chapter 11. In contrast, Mill argues from the psychological *fact* that most people want happiness to the conclusion that it is the appropriate ground for what we *ought* to do. His argument centres on a variation on Aristotle's claim that all people seek happiness as an ultimate end. He writes: "If the opinion which I have now stated is psychologically true – if human nature is so constituted as to desire nothing which is not either a part of happiness or a means of happiness – we can have no other proof, and we require no other, that these are the only things desirable."[11] This leads directly to his claim that the governing principle of all ethics ought to be "the greatest happiness of the greatest number".

This argument has been heavily criticized by many commentators, including those who are generally sympathetic to utilitarianism.[12] This very fact highlights an important element in critical thinking, namely that we can distinguish whether or not an *argument* is valid or *sound*, from the belief that the *conclusion* is *true*. If the argument is unsound, the conclusion has not been proved, but this does not mean that it is not true. If the emotivists, following the tradition of Hume, are right, the very notion of *proving* the truth of a moral claim in some factual way is a wholly mistaken enterprise.

If the emotivists are right on this matter, and J.S. Mill wrong, how then, could we demonstrate the correctness of a moral

---

[11] J.S.Mill, *Utilitarianism*, chapter 4.

[12] Mill's supporters sometimes argue that the problem can be avoided if we assume that Mill also has some unstated premises – which he assumed the reader would have in mind – perhaps something like: "We ought always to promote the courses of action that promote the greatest happiness of the greatest number".

philosophy? In wrestling with this question we anticipate some of the philosophies of the 20th century that will be outlined in chapter 11. If hard-line emotivism is correct, there is no answer (other than one that dismisses the validity of the question), because the very attempt to find a "proof" – at least one based on science or facts – is in itself to misunderstand the nature of moral thinking. On the other hand, if this means that making fundamental moral choices is simply a matter of – as it were – jumping on one bandwagon rather than another, this seems hugely to underestimate the way in which many human beings *ponder* ethical issues. This may be a helpful context for appreciating the very different, and very "rational" approach of Kant and the deontologists, which is outlined in the next chapter.

A reading from the introduction to J.S. Mill's *On Liberty* (1859)

The object of this Essay is to assert one very simple principle, as entitled to govern absolutely the dealings of society with the individual in the way of compulsion and control, whether the means be physical force in the form of legal penalties, or the moral coercion of public opinion. That principle is that the sole end for which mankind are warranted, individually or collectively, in interfering with the liberty of action of any of their number, is self-protection. That the only purpose for which power can be rightfully exercised over any member of a civilized community, against his will, is to prevent harm to others. His own good, either physical or moral, is not a sufficient warrant. He cannot rightfully be compelled to do or forbear because it will be better for him to do so, because it will make him happier, because in the opinion of others, to do so would be wise or even right. These are good reasons for remonstrating with him, or reasoning with him, or persuading him, or entreating him, but not for compelling him, or visiting him with any evil in case he do otherwise. The only part of the conduct of anyone for which he is amenable to society is that which concerns others. In the part which merely concerns himself, his independence is, of right, absolute. Over himself, over his own body and mind, the individual is sovereign.

Comment

This is a classic, perhaps *the* classic statement, of the right to personal liberty. In later paragraphs Mill adds some important qualifications.

(i) It does not apply to children, who are not yet able to make such decisions – and this leads to interesting questions about education, and at what age and in what measure young people should be free – in the opinion of others – to harm themselves. Education should be compulsory, Mill claims, because otherwise the parents are causing harm to the children; but this invites all kinds of questions concerning how much and what kind of education.

(ii) It does not apply to those with mental disease, who should be cared for by others, with their best long-term interests at heart – and this invites questions, for example, about how we draw the line between ordinary depression (which most people suffer from on occasions) and clinical depression, for which one can legally be put under the control of others.

In the main body of the essay *On Liberty*, and elsewhere, Mill discusses a number of other issues that arise, such as whether we should prevent people from taking drugs, whether they should be free to publish pornography, etc. In practice, it sometimes turns out that his principle of liberty is not quite as revolutionary as it might first appear, because all kinds of activities have indirect, but predictable consequences that cause harm to others, and therefore can be limited either by law or moral coercion. For example, he moved for an approval of laws that limit hours of labour and the unequal distribution of wealth, and both are issues where – in order to maximize the greatest happiness of the greatest number – some additional restrictions on liberty (in this case of the ruling classes) can be justified.

One of the complications is this: when we consider "harm" to others, to what extent do we mean *emotional* as distinct from *physical* harm? An anecdote from the U.K. can illustrate the point: A woman complained to the police that she was upset because members of a cult danced naked at the full moon outside her house, and this caused her mental distress. The police turned up and asked where the alleged offence occurred. They were taken to an upstairs bedroom window where the lady indicated a field some two hundred yards away. When the police said that this was not very close, she said "But I can see them very well through my telescope!" The police took the position that had the dancing been right under the window they would have acted (because there would have been predictable and unnecessary emotional harm to the lady), but in the circumstances they would do nothing. Clearly, the demand that we seek to prevent "harm" to others is capable of different interpretations!

Question 1

If a person is not mentally ill, should it be illegal for them to commit suicide on the grounds that they are harming no-one but themselves?

Comment

Some people argue that the mere fact that someone wants to commit suicide proves that they are mentally ill. This, I suggest, leads to a kind of circular argument.

Question 2

Just about every suicide causes at least mental (and often financial) harm to family members. Is this sufficient to bring it under Mill's principle?

Chapter 10. Kant and deontology

1. Empiricism and Rationalism

It will be helpful to place Kant's moral philosophy in a wider context. In introductory books on Western philosophy it is customary to contrast an Anglo-Saxon tradition, rooted in an empiricism that flourished in England and other English speaking countries, with a Continental tradition, rooted in what is sometimes called rationalism that flourished in the rest of Europe. The former is dominated by figures that include Francis Bacon, Thomas Hobbes, John Locke, George Berkeley, David Hume and J.S. Mill. The latter boasts figures that include Rene Descartes, Baruch Spinoza, Gottfried Leibniz, Immanuel Kant and Georg Hegel. Whereas a common theme of Anglo-Saxon philosophy was the empirical sciences, based on experiential knowledge as delivered through the five senses, the common theme of Continental philosophy was the use of what is called *a priori* reason. Locke's attack on innate ideas can be seen, in part, as an attack on this style of philosophizing.

The term *a priori* is a Latin term for "from before", meaning before (or prior to) empirical experience. This is in contrast to the Latin term *a posteriori*, meaning "from after" (or following) empirical experience. For example, mathematical knowledge is *a priori* because although – from the point of view of time – we may not have this knowledge until later in life, it is not based on empirical experience. Rather, it is based on mathematical reasoning that does not rely on observation of the world or on experimentation.

The distinction between the Anglo-Saxon and the rationalist (Continental) traditions is helpful provided we do not forget the huge differences between individual philosophers. The situation may remind us of the distinction between Western and Eastern philosophy, made in chapter 1, which, similarly, is only helpful if we see it in very general terms. We should also recall how the distinction between empiricism and rationalism mirrors tensions within ancient Greek philosophy. Plato, for example, not only thought that mathematics was the most noble of all the sciences, he also believed that reflective persons, through a process of "recollection", could discover certain truths that are already in what we might call the "unconscious mind". For this reason he could be classed as closer to the rationalist tradition, whereas Aristotle would be more aligned with the Anglo-Saxon, empiricist tradition.

2. Kant's Copernican Revolution

As in the case of Hobbes and Hume, we should understand the moral philosophy of Immanuel Kant (1724-1804) in the context of his more general philosophy, which he likened to the Copernican Revolution. Nicolaus Copernicus (1473-1543) was the great Polish scientist who provided the first conclusive evidence that the sun, not the earth, was the centre of the solar system. Some ancient astronomers, including Greeks, had suggested this sun-centred theory, but as a result of speculation rather than hard evidence. The gradual acceptance of the Copernican viewpoint had profound consequences on how people viewed fundamental questions in philosophy, because it seemed to lessen emphasis on human beings and their concerns. If the earth is not the centre of the universe, perhaps the human beings who inhabit it are not as significant as they think.

According to Kant, this scientific revolution in thinking is a metaphor for the way in which we all need to *reverse* how most of us think about knowledge. The common and naive view (as he saw it) was of a world external to us, but one that is sending information, through light and sound and other pathways, which conveys a more or less accurate picture of what it is like. In this model, our brains or minds are essentially *passive*, receiving this information through our five senses and processing it in some way to create the accurate picture. Even on this model, the brain does some processing (for example, our brains adjust our visual impressions to make things look the right way up), but Kant thinks that this processing is fundamental and radical. The world that we "see" is not an accurate picture of what is out there, it is an elaborate *construction*, formed by certain mental processes that are *a priori*. There is, Kant believed, a "world" out there, an ultimate reality that he called the *noumenal*; but we can have no direct access to it. What we have is what he termed the *phenomenal* world, meaning the world of appearances.

Superficially, this may remind us of the situation in Plato's Cave, where what people think is reality is actually a kind of illusion; but Kant's reasons for saying this are different from Plato's. In Plato you can envisage a situation whereby you gradually emerge from the cave and come to see reality. For Kant – at least while we are in our human bodies – this is impossible. In order to lead ordinary human lives, our minds structure the messages we receive, imposing factors that include space, time, and even causality. This is not the place to explore this interesting and highly controversial claim, but it can begin to explain how Kant sees the moral world; for here, Kant claims, we do gain some access to the noumenal realm. This is because we do not access the "good" by empirical means, but by rational ones. As a result, the radical internal processing that applies to factual information does not apply in this case. Here, therefore, there is an interesting agreement *and* disagreement with followers of Hume. The agreement is that both consider ethics not to be a matter of facts; the disagreement is that Hume and his followers conclude that morality is a matter of emotion or sentiment, while Kant sees it as a matter of rationality. Here we see Kant's link with the rationalist tradition.

3. The good will

The starting point for Kant's moral philosophy is his claim that the only thing that can be considered unequivocally good is the good will. He writes: "It is impossible to conceive anything at all in the world, or even out of it, which can be taken as good without qualification, except a good will. Intelligence, wit, judgement, and any other talents of the mind we may care to name, or courage, resolution, and constancy of purpose, as qualities of temperament, are without doubt good and desirable in many respects, but they can also be bad and hurtful when the will is not good which has to make use of these gifts of nature."[1] This means that when our will is good, all our actions are done *for the sake of duty*, and not for some other end, such as our own happiness. In other words, from a moral perspective, we ought to act simply because this is the right thing to do, not because we have some inclination – a sentiment of sympathy or a desire to maximize the greatest happiness of the greatest number.

It is easy to misunderstand what Kant claims here. Suppose that, out of a feeling of love or sympathy, I visit my lonely grandmother. Kant would not say that this is wrong; indeed he would probably say that my action is in accordance with duty. I have done the right thing,

---

[1] Immanuel Kant, *Groundwork of the Metaphysic of Morals*, in the H.J. Paton translation of 1947 (London: Hutchinson University Library) and republished since.

Kant and deontology

but nevertheless, he would say that the action has no moral worth because I did not do it from duty alone.

Whether or not we agree with Kant, we can see that he is making an important point. Consider the case of someone who has two options regarding the next half hour, and that she has a strong inclination to do one of two things: She would like either to buy an ice cream and enjoy it while sitting on a park bench, or visit her lonely grandmother who lives next door. She enjoys the prospect of doing either – it is not a case of possibly visiting her grandmother purely out of duty, but because of the pleasure of the conversation and the nice cup of tea that will be provided. Eventually, weighing up the two "inclinations", she decides to visit her grandmother. Kant would probably say that she has done the right thing or that she has acted "in accordance with duty", but that the action is no more worthy of moral praise than if she had opted for the ice cream. She has simply opted to follow one inclination instead of another. Next, suppose she is the kind of religious person who believes that good deeds, such as visiting her grandmother (even if a boring experience) will be rewarded by God – perhaps with good luck or a quicker access to heaven – and that this leads her to visit the grandmother. Again Kant would say: "You've done the right thing, but there is no moral worth. If God rewards good deeds in this way, this would be no different from God rewarding you for eating that ice cream." According to Kant, if there are rewards, they must be totally independent of our motive or inclination. Some people would say that the rewards could be the consequence of being the kind of person that we are, but never the motive.

Here we need to make another diversion into a religious issue, since it impacts on ethics. The crude message of some preachers, especially in the monotheistic religions, is that being good is a matter of seeking rewards in heaven; but this is a caricature of these religions at their best. The proper motive for doing good deeds – according to the founders of these religions – should be love or compassion, not the reward. Indeed, in this context, the very word "motive" may be inappropriate. Benefit for us, in some cases, might be a *consequence*, but it cannot be a motive. How could it be a consequence? There is a clue in the earlier reference to the result of being a certain kind of person. In Plato's *Republic*, those who do evil damage their own souls, and so a kind of negative consequence is automatic. In the Hindu concept of *karma*, all that we do has an effect on our souls and therefore our capacity for happiness. In the teaching of Jesus we should love God because he loves us, and so on.

Kant's insistence on acting out of duty has a certain resonance with Aristotle's account of *hexis* – his word for an *acquired* virtue or disposition. We saw, in chapter 4, that a *hexis* is developed by force of habit, typically by being made to do things when young, or choosing to do things when more mature, that are not in accordance with our inclinations. Here, there is both a similarity and a great gulf between the philosophies of Kant and of Aristotle. The similarity is that personal pleasure should not be, and in a sense cannot be, what drives virtuous persons. The gulf is this. For Aristotle, once you have developed a virtue, the fact that you enjoy doing a good deed (that is, acting in accordance with your virtuous disposition), is an indication that you are a good person. For Kant, this is totally irrelevant. Indeed the presence of such pleasure probably indicates that there is no moral worth.[2] This can be illustrated by the following scenario:

---

[2] The situation is complicated by the fact that – according to Kant – the mere presence of pleasure does not prove that the act was not done from a sense of duty. It might just happen to be the case that you acted both in accordance with duty and for the sake of duty, and – at the same time – just happened, by good fortune, to gain pleasure from the act.

Nurse A works in an old people's home, caring for the sick and dying, and she does so not because she enjoys it, but because she feels an obligation or sense of duty to act in this way. Nurse B acts – outwardly – in exactly the same way, but – because she is a person of great empathy – actually enjoys the work. According to Kant, both nurses are acting (in all probability) in accordance with duty, but only nurse A has moral worth, because she acts from a sense of duty, not inclination. According to Aristotle, although both nurses (probably) are acting in accordance with duty (this is not an expression that Aristotle uses), it is only nurse B who demonstrates virtue – because once we have developed a virtue, one of the signs of maturity is that the virtuous action is both natural and pleasurable. This – in my view – is an interesting way of bringing out two very different, but also two understandable, versions of moral merit.

What then enables the good person, according to Kant, to be "moved" to do the right thing? It cannot be any kind of inclination, or the problem of preferring the visit to grandmothers to eating ice-cream returns (or so Kant would claim). Here, once again, we recall Plato and his notion of the two horses (representing passions) and the charioteer (representing reason). According to Kant, human beings have a strange capacity for responding to what he calls "reverence" (German *achtung*) for the moral law. This, he insists, is not a special kind of inclination, but some kind of rational quality, by which we can choose to reverence and then respond to a sense of duty, simply because it is recognized as a duty.

Needless to say, this Kantian position on the ability of sheer reason (backed by a "reverence" that is very hard not to describe as some special kind of "inclination"), is highly controversial. It may be said that the issue raised – namely, what kinds of passion, or reason, or whatever, can move us towards the good – is one of the abiding questions in moral philosophy, and on this matter there is no universal agreement.

4. The categorical imperative

According to Kant, how do I know what is my duty? His answer is as famous and as important as his claim about the good will. The question we have continually to ask ourselves is: "Can the maxim (the word used by most translations for our personal principle or ground for action) according to which I propose to act, be universalized?" Consider Kant's example of lying. A man is pondering whether to tell a lie in order to get out of financial difficulty. The principle (or maxim) on which a man proposes to lie goes: "Whenever I believe myself short of money, I will borrow money and promise to pay it back, though I know it will never be done." Ethically, the key question is: can this principle (or maxim) be universalized – that is to say – made into the kind of universal law that everyone could consistently follow? Kant says "No", and his argument is more subtle than is often realized. The point is not the obvious one that if the liar were himself lied to, he would be annoyed. Similarly, if I am a burglar and I find myself burgled, I will very likely be highly annoyed, showing inconsistency. While this is true, it is incidental to the main argument. The key point is this: if people generally acted on a principle that they can lie for their own self-interest, there would be a logical contradiction to its universalization. This is because our very ability to lie depends upon a general sense of trust. If this trust did not exist then no-one could lie successfully. They could not in fact *deceive* people because the very act of deception depends on a context in which people generally tell the truth. So an act of lying is *parasitic* on everyone else telling the truth. Therefore, rationally, I cannot universalize the principle upon which I or anyone else told a lie.

This argument helps to explain one of the ways in which Kant describes the fundamental moral law – the one that he calls the "categorical imperative". You must act only on a principle that you can universalize, a principle that could be a universal law that everyone always followed.

5. Three problems

Kant's position has been of huge influence, but it is not without its problems. Every moral philosophy that we have examined raises problems that are not easy to answer, and the significance of this will be considered in the final chapter. Three of these problems are indicated in this section.

(i) The white lie. Notoriously Kant thought he had proved that lying is *always* wrong, even if it is to save someone's life.[3] However, what he has in fact proved (I would argue) is that one cannot rationally universalize the principle: "I will tell a lie for the sake of my self-interest". I cannot see that this must rule out all "white lies", told, let us say, to save the innocent. A classic example is that of a Dutch farmer who, in 1943, hid Jews in his barn in order to protect them from the German secret police. When asked if he was hiding Jews he replied "No" (and while the police were looking in his neighbour's barns, he quietly moved them to a safer place, thereby saving their lives). If the principle (maxim) here was: "I can tell a lie on those rare occasions when it is necessary to save innocent lives", this would not destroy the general trust which provides the context for being believed. If I am right, the question of exactly

---

[3] Strangely, in his *Lectures on Ethics*, Kant does make one very odd exception, concerning self-protection. (*Lectures on Ethics*, section on "Ethical Duties towards Others: Truthfulness".) However, in his essay of 1797, *On a supposed right to lie from altruistic motives*, he denies that one should tell a lie to save someone else from murder.

what the principle is that can or cannot be universalized is not as straightforward as Kant thought.

(ii) The suicide bomber. According to Kant's moral philosophy the typical suicide bomber is not only *acting* wrongly (that is to say, he is not acting in accordance with duty), but also without good intent or good will. This is because the motive is some reward, such as a place in heaven. However, we have to face the fact that a small proportion of suicide bombers (and some other people we often call fanatics) are not acting for this reason, but because they honestly believe that they are doing the right thing. If they are acting solely because they believe that this terrible action is the right thing to do, then, according to the Kantian philosophy, even though they have acted wrongly, that is to say, not in accordance with duty, they may, nevertheless, have acted "for the sake of duty". If that is so then, according to Kantian philosophy, they have moral merit. This is a worrying and paradoxical conclusion because it clashes with our basic sense of what is good and bad. It may also remind us of an analogous, and ancient, problem with regard to "conscience". If following one's conscience means doing what one honestly believes is right, then all kinds of terrible actions, including many acts of religious persecution, start to look as if (however mistaken) the actors have moral merit.

My own view, which I have discussed elsewhere,[4] involves a criticism of the Kantian view, effectively claiming that it needs to be set within a wider discussion concerning the nature of the good. In addition to the demand to endeavour to follow the good, as we see it, I suggest we also have a responsibility to develop some coherent notion of what the good is. This is to be found, at least in part,

---

[4] Michael J. Langford, *The Tradition of Liberal Theology* (Grand Rapids: Eerdmans, 2014), pp. 85-6.

through Aristotle's emphasis on the need to acquire genuine virtue through how we manage our *whole* lives, which will hugely affect how we define the good. It also resonates with Aristotle's claim that we have the potentiality to respond to the "eye for the good" with which the virtuous person is endowed by nature.[5] I am not suggesting that such considerations "solve" the problem of the unselfish suicide bomber, but they may begin to point us towards a more comprehensive account of the moral order.

With respect to the absolute duty – allegedly – to follow our consciences, there is a long tradition, especially within Catholic theology, of making careful distinctions between "conscience" in the sense of the immediate feeling of what is right and wrong; and "conscience" in the sense of a considered and thoughtful reflection on what is right and wrong. Once again, while this does not solve all the problems, it may begin to steer us towards a more subtle and comprehensive moral philosophy.

(iii) Utilitarianism by the back door. How do we decide whether or not a particular kind of action can be universalized? Consider again the case of lying. If I ask myself, "What would happen if everyone acted in this way – that is by telling lies?", then it might seem that I am actually using a calculation of consequences as the criterion for what is right and wrong. If that is so, far from Kantian deontology being a different approach to that of utilitarianism, it is actually dependent on it. Utilitarian considerations are, as it were, brought in by the back door. Most Kantians strongly resist this suggestion, arguing that the kind of *rational* evaluation of what can or cannot be universalized is essentially a different kind of process. It seems to me that at least from a psychological point of view they are

---

[5] Aristotle, *Nicomachean Ethics*, 1114a-b.

right. But if the result turns out to be the same, or almost the same, as if we had calculated the consequences, then questions arise as to whether utilitarianism (especially in Mill's more moderate version) can be contrasted with deontology as strongly as Kant thought.

6. Two positive features of Kantianism

Many readers of this survey of Western moral philosophy will feel that although there are problems with all the great philosophers we have considered, nevertheless, all of them have made some important contributions to the tradition of moral thinking. Indeed, if this were not so, it is unlikely that they would have become as influential as they have. In the case of Kant I want to suggest what two of these positive features are so that even if we are not prepared to be *Kantians* (essentially, viewing moral philosophy in the way that he did), we can see that he has – as it were – put his finger on these insights.

(i) Accepting one's common humanity, rather than treating oneself as an exception. Kant's *categorical imperative* – his equivalent of Mill's *supreme principle of morality* – is expressed, by him, in several different ways.[6] The one that we have examined so far goes like this: "Always act according to a principle [maxim] that you can universalize". It has also been formulated in this way: "Make sure that the principle on which you act could be a universal law for all human beings." I have suggested that one way of understanding these formulations is to realize how an act of wrongdoing is – as it were – *parasitic* on society. Here, I suggest, Kant has indeed put his finger on something that truly resonates with how nearly all of us feel

---

[6] Commentators disagree about whether these different formulations of the categorical imperative are (as Kant seemed to believe) essentially different ways of saying the same thing, or whether they actually introduce different moral claims.

Kant and deontology

about morality, because the person we want to criticize is typically the person who treats themselves as an exception to the rules. A game of football can only take place if all, or almost all, players follow the rules. The few who break the rules need to be dealt with in a consistent way by the referee; otherwise, the whole game will fall apart. Similarly it can be argued that "the great game of life" depends on nearly all of us, nearly all of the time, obeying the rules that make human society viable. For example, if rules that restrict violence within the community are not generally observed, we may lapse into a Hobbesian state of nature.[7]

I shall revisit this point in the discussion of H.L.A. Hart in the last chapter. This philosopher regards the rules that make human society viable as a kind of minimum content for a basic natural or universal moral law. Hart argued that Aristotle's natural justice and Aquinas' natural law are not altogether mistaken ideas.

In this matter of wrongdoing being associated with treating oneself as an exception, Kant, I suggest, has indeed put his finger on a central aspect of how nearly all of us feel about morality. The habitual burglar, person of violence, tax cheat, etc. is someone whom we dislike and condemn because they are not accepting the rules that bind us together and make our human societies viable. We may feel outraged because most of us – at least tacitly – have agreed to follow the rules, even when it is difficult to do so.

(ii) Ends in themselves. In the last section I described two slightly different formulations of Kant's categorical imperative. Both are categorical, he insists, because they command absolutely, with no implicit "if". In contrast, a *hypothetical imperative* goes like this: "Do x if you want to achieve y." Precisely because Kant is what is

---

[7] Violence outside the community, as in tribal warfare, also raises moral questions, but not in the sense that without them there cannot be a community.

called a deontologist (where duty is not dependent on matters such as sentiment or consequences), moral imperatives are categorical. Hence, they can be stated as "Do x, regardless."

Another way in which Kant describes his categorical imperative goes: "Always treat every person as an end in themselves, and not as a mere means." In order to understand what he is saying consider the following scenario: I have a desire to meet the Prime Minister, and I know that my acquaintance, Jones, is one of his friends. I get close to Jones, pretending to befriend him, and then persuade him to introduce me to the Prime Minister. He does so, and then I immediately drop my friendship with Jones, even though he had wanted to be my friend. In this scenario I have *used* Jones, rather like a "mere means" or a commodity might be used; and not – Kant would say – treated him as a person. We must note that the word "mere" is important. If Jones were really my friend, and I asked him to do me a favour, such as introducing me to the Prime Minister, he would be a "means", but not a "mere means". Other things being the same, Kant would have no objection to this. Quite often, and quite properly, our friends are a means to our happiness.

This suggestion about not treating people as "mere" means has many important and, I suggest, helpful applications. In sexual relations, for example, it can mark a huge and morally significant difference between, on the one hand, consensual sex between two adults who both really want this kind of intimacy; and on the other hand, exploitative situations where either party (and sometimes both) are *used* as if they were commodities. Another application is in business relations, especially between management level and worker, where it is easy for relationships to become one-sided and exploitative. In working out the implications of Kant's principle: "Treat everyone as an end in themselves", we can find one of the

A reading from Kant's *Lectures on Ethics*[8]

Those who advocate suicide seek to give the widest interpretation to freedom. There is something flattering in the thought that we can take our own life if we are so minded; and so we find even right-thinking persons defending suicide in this respect. There are many circumstances under which life ought to be sacrificed. If I cannot preserve my life except by violating my duties towards myself, I am bound to sacrifice my life rather than violate these duties. But suicide is in no circumstances permissible. Humanity in one's own person is something inviolable; it is a holy trust; a man is master of all else, but he must not lay hands upon himself .....

But suicide is not inadmissible and abominable because God has forbidden it; God has forbidden it because it is abominable in that it degrades man's inner worth below that of the animal creation.

Question

Is Kant right to argue that suicide, in all circumstances, is wrong?

Comment

In the case of lying, we distinguished the maxim: "I can lie for the sake of my self-interest" (which, I suggest, Kant is right to say cannot be universalized), from the maxim: "I can tell a lie in order to preserve someone from great harm" (which, I suggest, is not so problematic). Similarly, we could distinguish a maxim: "I can take

---

[8] These are lecture notes taken by Kant's students. We gratefully acknowledge Taylor and Francis for permission to quote in chapter 10 from *Immanuel Kant: Lectures on Ethics*. (Louis Infield translator). London: Methuen, 1930, p.151.

my own life when I find it convenient to do so" (which would almost certainly cause pain to others, and which Kant clearly thinks is to violate a duty to ourselves) from another maxim: "I can take my own life when it is necessary to protect other people". An example of the latter would be a spy who chooses to kill himself rather than be tortured, when he knows that under torture he will betray his friends. It is one thing to say that suicide is generally wrong (a position that can be argued from utilitarian as well as Kantian grounds); it is another thing to say it is wrong in all conceivable circumstances.

Chapter 11. The contemporary scene

Background

In many cultures, throughout long periods of time, some philosophies have represented ideas and values shared by most, if not all, people. If we take a world-wide perspective, it is doubtful whether this is now the case. One of the interesting questions that emerges is whether or not some kind of global worldview (with a moral philosophy that is at least implicit) would be a good thing – perhaps one that included strong emphases on matters such as the equality of women, the rights of the oppressed, and the ecological protection of this planet. These, of course, are in themselves practical issues rather than meta-ethical issues; but a commonly-shared position on them is likely to be much easier if there is some shared moral philosophy.[1]

In many cultures there has been a generally accepted moral philosophy, although there have always been radicals or heretics who have not agreed with the prevailing philosophy. For example, in the Middle Ages the moral philosophy of Thomas Aquinas was generally accepted throughout Western Europe, at least in terms

---

[1] J.S. Mill, for example, supported women's equality because, in his view, this would increase overall happiness, and more specifically because it was one of those aspects of liberty that was at the heart of most people's sense of wellbeing. Some deontologists would take a stronger line, arguing that this utilitarian argument left women's rights vulnerable to a claim that in some cultures adopting these alleged rights might undermine overall happiness, perhaps because of problems regarding social stability.

of its general principles. In the intellectual coffee houses of 18th century France, the convictions of the *philosophes* – while not as widely accepted as Aquinas in the Middle Ages – represented widely held positions. The contemporary scene, however, is much more diverse. Both professional philosophers and the general public hold, either explicitly or implicitly, a huge variety of positions, although on some practical issues there is often a consensus. For example, most Westerners believe in freedom of speech (though often with qualifications) and a welfare system that protects the poor and the vulnerable (though the level of its generosity is debated). In terms of moral philosophy or meta-ethics there is no consensus. In the following sections I shall indicate the range of positions held by contemporary philosophers, yet even this extensive list will not be exhaustive.

In chapter 4 we noted that students of moral philosophy are often taught that there are three main types of moral philosophy: utilitarianism, which we examined in chapter 8; deontology, which we examined in chapter 9; and virtue ethics, which is said to begin with Aristotle, whose thought we explored in chapter 4. We also noted that the restriction to these types of philosophy is very misleading because, especially since the time of Hume, the situation is far more diverse. In the contemporary scene these three streams of thought are still very much alive, although in many different versions. I shall begin the list of contemporary theories with versions of these three traditions.

1. Virtue ethics

An influential example of one contemporary version of virtue ethics is provided in the writings of the Scottish philosopher Alasdair MacIntyre (born in 1929). He started with a variation on Marxist thought, but moved to a secular version of Aristotle's virtue ethics[2] and subsequently to a position that echoes the thought of Aquinas and sets virtue ethics within a more metaphysical context – emphasizing the importance of accepting the notion of a teleology even more than before. We may recall that many philosophers, including Plato, have changed their minds during the course of their lives.

After Virtue admits the massive disagreement that exists among philosophers and also the many different notions of what it is to be rational. This is signified by the very title of another of MacIntyre's books, *Whose Justice? Which Rationality?* The contemporary scene, he argues, is marked by disorder, a disorder that results from the failure of Enlightenment philosophers, and those that immediately followed them, to transcend either the individualism or the emotivism that marred their thinking. In particular – MacIntyre continues – we cannot make sense of ethics without appreciating, not so much what we are as where we come from. With regard to the disorder and chaos in attempts to find a common rationality, he does, in the end, allow for criteria by which one form of rationality might properly be preferred to others – in terms of overall coherence and practicality. This fits with his claim that the disagreements we encounter do not force us to an overall relativism.

Here, some further explanation is needed. Every thoughtful person agrees that some moral claims are relative to the cultures in which they are found. We may recall that the ancient Greeks often discussed the moral variations that were highlighted by travellers' tales concerning strange customs in other lands. Nevertheless, Socrates, Plato and Aristotle, in different ways, all argued that there were some universal standards (as in Aristotle's natural justice). This

---

[2] Notably in *After Virtue* (3rd ed. London: Duckworth, 2007).

"natural justice" (more or less equivalent to Aquinas' natural law) has a kind of universal authority rooted in what is claimed to be required for human flourishing. It is to be contrasted with "conventional justice", which, like the term "positive morality" refers to what is valued in a particular culture, and is subject to much variation. When people refer to relativism, sometimes they are referring quite simply to this local, conventional justice which is relative to local conditions, but sometimes they mean something much more strident and controversial, namely the claim that *all* justice is conventional and relative to local cultures. This, for example, was the view of some Sophists. MacIntyre totally rejects this more strident form of relativism.

We could also put the issue this way. In extreme relativism, nothing is truly right or wrong, and the words *right* and *wrong* only refer to local customs or feelings. In what I call "moderate" relativism, the significance of local, positive morality is acknowledged. But it is allowed, nevertheless, that there is also a universal morality required for human flourishing. According to this universal morality many things are *really wrong* – even if it is much harder to say what things are *really right*. To put this in another way: in the case of many practical issues (such as how we ought to punish murderers), there may not be one obviously "correct" answer, but there are certainly wrong answers – such as those that demand torture.

We saw in chapter 4 that the word "teleology" comes from the Greek word *telos*, meaning an end or purpose. As soon as we admit the possibility of human beings having a purpose that goes beyond that of their own choosing, we return to what might be termed a "robust" version of virtue ethics, one that invites a modern version of Aristotle or Aquinas to be taken seriously.

Important sections of *After Virtue* discuss and dismiss the alternative reaction to intellectual disorder provided by the German philosopher Friedrich Nietzsche (1844-1900). Whereas Nietzsche advocated a return to a kind of Homeric ethic,[3] with its emphasis on the inherent superiority of an aristocratic "superman" (German *ubermensch*), MacIntyre seeks a return to a kind of communitarianism, in which the social virtues become the guide to what morality is really about.

2. Utilitarianism

As we saw in chapter 9, all forms of utilitarianism, by definition, are consequentialist, and all make "utility" the criterion of what is useful. In other ways, however, they vary. Indeed, we saw that even in the case of "classical utilitarianism" the positions of Bentham and J.S. Mill are very different. Utilitarianism is still a popular moral theory, and in this section we shall mention just *one* of its present supporters, the Australian philosopher Peter Singer (born in 1946).

Singer's variation is sometimes called "preference utilitarianism". For self-conscious persons, he argues, the consequences that maximize the interests (or preferences) of people most effectively is what ought to be pursued, regardless of whether this is likely to achieve more happiness for them. For others, including animals, it is what will maximize their pleasure. Although Singer's early writings sometimes expressed a suspicion of any rational evaluation of moral principles, in his later writings he supports the view that there are rational grounds for preferring

---

[3] Homer probably composed his poems around 700 BCE. *The Iliad* and *The Odyssey* are set during the Trojan War and its aftermath, and were the poems every Greek philosopher took seriously. The poems describe a world where honour and military valour are the outstanding virtues.

the impartial standpoint of J.S. Mill's utilitarianism – that is to say – to place the greatest happiness of the greatest number above that of our own personal happiness. Of considerable interest and influence is his book *Animal Liberation* (1975)[4], which builds upon Bentham's emphasis on how the crucial factor in considering our treatment of animals is that they can suffer. In his view, animals have as much right to be considered in the calculation of consequences as human beings, and he uses the term *speciesism* to contrast the proper utilitarian point of view to that of most moralists. They (following Aristotle) have paid little regard to the issue of animal suffering. This view has led Singer to support both vegetarianism and veganism, but it has not led him to object to *all* animal experimentation – provided that the likely benefits of the proposed research clearly outweigh the limited suffering to which the animals are exposed.

A comment on the relationship of utilitarianism to vegetarianism can help to indicate an interesting ambiguity within utilitarianism philosophies. Many supporters of animal rights and, more generally, of a more humane treatment of animals, avoid a utilitarian standpoint because of the following problem.

In our assessment of consequences, should we consider the potential happiness of lives that do not yet exist, and might not come to exist if we adopt a certain policy? Take the case of sheep that live out in the fields. It is reasonable to argue that most of the time they enjoy some quality of life. (The situations of caged chickens, force-fed geese and young cows penned in to produce veal are very different.) If all of us became vegetarians, only a few sheep would be kept (as pets, or in zoos, or for their wool) and therefore – the argument seems to imply – there would be far less "sheep

---

[4] Peter Singer, *Animal Liberation* (3rd ed. London: Pimlico, 1995)

happiness", since even if the conditions of slaughter are negative, the overall life of most sheep is probably positive. It seems likely, therefore, that utilitarian arguments, by themselves, are unlikely to support vegetarianism with respect to sheep. However, this is only because I have put into the equation the sheep that may or may not exist in the future as a result of my present choices. Whether or not utilitarian calculations should do this is itself an interesting issue. Similar questions arise in debates over abortion, where the potential happiness of the unborn may or may not be included in the calculation, according to the kind of utilitarianism that is proposed. The English philosopher Derek Parfit (1942–2017) has helped to draw attention to this issue for moral philosophy.

A similar question concerning the interpretation of utilitarianism can be expressed like this: Are we concerned with the average happiness of sentient beings, or the overall sum of happiness? If the latter, then huge numbers of sentient beings, each just barely happy, might be preferable to having fewer, but intensely happy, sentient beings. How should this choice be made?

3. Kant and Rawls

The philosophy of Kant continues to influence philosophy, and one of the foremost proponents of a Kantian ethical and political philosophy is the Harvard professor John Rawls (1921-2002), in particular through his book *A Theory of Justice* (1971)[5]. In order to decide rationally what kind of political order we should encourage and support, Rawls recommends a thought experiment. We imagine ourselves about to arrive on this planet but "behind a veil of ignorance" concerning where and how we will be born. In

---

[5] John Rawls, *A Theory of Justice* (revised edition. Oxford: Oxford University Press, 1999)

this situation, he argues, it would be rational to support a kind of universal justice, in which there is the greatest overall fairness, and no such institution as slavery. In this way, the rational agent is likely to support fairness between the sexes, economic classes, religious positions, the abled and disabled, etc. Also, he argues, it would be rational to support what he calls the *difference principle.* Political programmes that assist the richer classes can only be supported if they also, at the same time, bring some added benefit to the poorer classes. They must succeed in making some positive "difference" to the lives of the less advantaged. This suggestion raises interesting questions. For example, some people argue that if a programme strongly benefits the rich and only slightly benefits the poor, this might be a *bad* thing, because even though the poor are now better off than they would have been, the result is a still greater divide between the rich and the poor. Even from a purely utilitarian point of view, this may be problematic. For example, it may bring about more instability and violence. As a result, Rawls' difference principle is not universally accepted.

There are other problems with Rawls' approach. Let us suppose that I am a risk taker and while behind the veil of ignorance I decide to opt for a very unjust society in the hope that I will be born into a rich family, perhaps that of a Roman patrician. Rawls would probably say that this would be very irrational, since there was a greater chance that I might be a slave. However, if that is so, hasn't Rawls – as it were – sneaked in his idea of a rational decision into the assumed character of the person making a decision behind the veil of ignorance? The decision has become the one he thinks (perhaps rightly) that I ought to make, not necessarily the one I would make.

Despite these difficulties, I suggest that Rawls has produced an interesting, and potentially helpful, way in which some people may be able to think about issues of justice. Standing back and asking ourselves questions as if we were in the veil of ignorance may well produce some creative ideas.

4. Emotivism

Although the roots of emotivism go back to Hume's emphasis on sympathy (and indeed earlier, because some ancient Greeks stressed the importance of the emotions in the moral life), the term "emotivism" is often restricted to some of the moral philosophies that emerged in the 1930s. A somewhat crude, but for a time popular version, appeared in A.J. Ayer's *Language, Truth, and Logic* (1936)[6], where it is insisted that moral expressions have no reference to facts, they simply express or evince emotion. This book is also famous for its claim that moral philosophy should make no ethical pronouncements at all – for philosophers, as philosophers, should only be concerned with the most general issues in meta-ethics. Practical ethics – just because it is simply the "evincing" of emotions – has nothing to do with rational argument. Most emotivists have had more subtle accounts of moral language, rooted in both negative and positive arguments. Essentially, the principal negative argument goes like this. When someone claims that something is good, we should ask: "Is this 'good' a 'natural quality', capable of some empirical confirmation?" It might seem that it cannot be, and one reason is that (as the philosopher G.E. Moore pointed out[7]), whatever "natural" feature we consider (such as being red or heavy) may not be considered good in some circumstances. Perhaps then, "good" refers

---

[6] A.J. Ayer, *Language, Truth and Logic* (2nd ed. London: Gollancz, 1946)

[7] G.E. Moore, *Principia Ethica* (1903; rev. ed. Cambridge: Cambridge University Press, 1993)

to some "non-natural" property, but this seemed to most philosophers such a strange kind of "property" that few accepted the suggestion. Most decided that value terms do not refer to *any* property or relation. However, more important is a kind of positive argument for an emotivist position, found in writers such as Charles Stevenson[8]. Any adequate analysis of the word "good", he insists, must fulfil three requirements. First, it should make it possible for us to disagree (since we obviously do so on many occasions). Second, "good" must have a kind of "magnetism", since whenever something is alleged to be good we recognize that there is a suggestion being made in its favour. The statement of value does not so much present a fact, as create an influence. Third, the analysis should not make the issue of goodness a mere question of empirical fact (as in many neutral-free statements).[9]

It should be clear from this brief summary that emotivism is closely associated with theories concerning the use of language, and with what is known as the school of analytic philosophy that has flourished in many British and American universities since the 1930s. In the case of many emotivist philosophers, the old division between Anglo-Saxon empiricism and Continental rationalism is still evident. The typical approach to ethics within the analytic tradition, rooted in the analysis of language, is a manifestation of this. At its worst, this means a rather boring and technical analysis of sentences. At its best, it means a clarification of terms that can then lead to a much more informed discussion of fundamental issues. Also, to their credit (whatever one's ultimate assessment of them may be) emotivist theories illuminate many subtle ways in which moral

---

[8] Charles Stevenson, *Ethics and Language* (New Haven: Yale University Press, 1944)
[9] See J.O. Urmson, *The Emotive Theory of Ethics* (London: Hutchinson, 1968), p. 22.

language actually works.[10] It is far more than a bland reference to the emotional source of our values.

On several occasions, we have noted that while simple definitions often suggest hard lines between rival theories, more subtle accounts of different philosophies frequently blur the distinctions – a good example being the supposed hard line between utilitarianism and deontology. Another example is provided by the emphasis on "attitudes", found in many of the more subtle accounts of emotivism, such as that of Charles Stevenson. The more we consider attitudes that, in turn, lead to consistent patterns of behaviour, the more we seem to be straying into the field of virtue ethics.

A word should be added concerning the philosophy of Ludwig Wittgenstein (1891-1951), the Austrian-born philosopher who taught at Cambridge and whose accounts of how language is used has been of major influence. While only a small part of his writings concern ethics, they are famous for the claim that ethical language is nonsense. However, he also says that he respects rather than condemns those who use it.[11] He appears to have a similar approach to religious language. What are we to make of these two different elements regarding ethics? The clue lies in the difference between "nonsense", meaning what is trivial or meaningless, and "non-sense", meaning "not a matter of empirical fact". Thus there is common ground with A.J. Ayer and the emotivists in distancing all value language from factual language. But – in his deep respect for moral discourse – there is a vast difference from Ayer, and from some,

---

[10] I am thinking, in particular, of the work of the English philosopher J.L. Austin, 1911-1960.

[11] E.g. at the close of his "Lecture on Ethics" - translated in *The Philosophical Review*. Vol. 74 (1965), p.5 - where he says that the desire to say something about matters such as the meaning of life "can be no science" and yet it represents a tendency in the human mind "which I personally cannot help respecting deeply". Cf. his comments on p. 16.

but not all emotivists. Ethics, for Wittgenstein, is a special kind of domain of discourse – or (in his own terms) a different kind of "language game". This ought to be taken with the utmost seriousness. For Wittgenstein, ethics is among the things that can be "shown", but not described.

5. Moral realism

In stark contrast to emotivism we find a revival, among some philosophers, of what is termed "moral realism". Three claims underlie the statements that are typically made by those who use this term: (i) there are moral "truths" or "facts"; (ii) these truths are independent of our particular beliefs, and, consequently; (iii) we can be mistaken about these truths. The alleged moral "facts" are not, of course, empirical, in the sense that they can be directly observed by the senses. Given the way in which, for so many people, the word "fact" is anchored in what can be empirically observed, I think it better to think of moral realism as the insistence that there are moral *truths*, rather than moral *facts*.

An influential exponent of moral realism was the British philosopher Philippa Foot (1920-2010) who, notwithstanding the arguments of the emotivists, defended a version of naturalism. The emotivists, using an argument developed by the philosopher G.E. Moore, labelled any identification of value with a natural fact "the naturalistic fallacy". However, the "facts" Foot claimed to be foundational for ethics are of a special kind. They are the truths about human nature – such as our potentials and vulnerabilities, and our need for relationships – that make it possible for human life to flourish. These are, in an important sense, *contingent* facts, dependent not on necessary truths, but on what we actually find to be the human condition. Therefore, empirical observation does enter the picture in a crucial way. Foot argued that there is an intimate connection between natural facts and ethics[12]. Jokingly, this has led some people to refer to "the naturalistic fallacy fallacy".

As so often in moral philosophy, there is no sharp division between Foot's version of naturalism and virtue ethics, of which she was also a major proponent[13].

6. Marxist and Neo-Marxist theories

In chapter 5 and 7 we discussed two very different kinds of materialism. One refers to the ultimate nature of all reality, while the other refers to "egoism" – the kind of materialism that goes with the accumulation of wealth for our personal benefit. Hobbes, I pointed out, was a materialist in both senses. The German philosopher Karl Marx (1818-1883), as with the Stoics, was a materialist in the first, but not the second sense. Just as Hobbes had his own version of materialism (an emphasis on laws of motion rather than some kind of ultimate building block), so did Marx. In addition to a rejection of the kind of spiritual ultimate reality that was proposed by Hegel, Marx claimed that the ultimate driving force for all historical movements was the economic conditions in which human beings are placed. In the short run, he admitted, other factors, such as the influence of dynamic personalities, might be of consequence. But the longer the view we take, the more the ultimate explanations of all history are seen in terms of the material conditions described by economic science. This book is not concerned with Marx's economic philosophy as such, except insofar as it helps to explain his moral philosophy, but it is concerned with his rejection of the egoistic

---

[12] Philippa Foot, "Does Moral Subjectivism Rest on a Mistake?". *Oxford Journal of Legal Studies*. Vol. 15 (1995), pp.1-14.

[13] Philippa Foot: *Virtues and Vices* (Oxford: Blackwell, 1978)

materialism. The clue to his approach can be found in his early *Philosophical Manuscripts*. According to Marx, a human person is, by nature, a "species-being"; and he claims that communism, when properly understood, is "the true solution of the conflict between existence and essence".[14]

As is well known, Marx thought that the solution to human problems was a revolution in which the lowest economic level of society gained power – in the name of all – and that would then be the end of the historical spiral of political change. Once the proletariat came to power there would no longer be an underclass waiting to supplant them. Once in power, he believed, there would be a gradual evolution to true communism (replacing the dictatorship of the proletariat that immediately succeeded the revolution), and alienation would diminish. Alienation is a central concept in Marx's ethics, and – he claims – becomes progressively worse under capitalist systems. It encompasses alienation of one person from another, of persons from nature and from the products of their activity, and – in a subtle sense – even from their true selves. In principle, all these forms of alienation can be overcome once we have a classless society in which oppression disappears.[15]

---

[14] In his *Economic and Philosophical Manuscripts*, Marx describes how, when man is properly liberated, he can find his true nature as "a species being"; that is to say, as a person who can only be truly fulfilled when he discovers his co-operative place within human society. See Erich Fromm, *Marx's Concept of Man*, which includes a translation of his *Economic and Philosophical Manuscripts* (New York: Frederick Ungar Publishing, 1961), p. 102. On communism as the true solution, see p. 127. Teachings such as these have led at least one significant philosopher to place Marx within the tradition of (secular) natural law. See Hans Kelsen, *The Communist Theory of Law* (London: Stevens, 1955).

[15] The concept of alienation in Marx has strong similarities with the Christian concept of sin, which similarly alienates persons from each other and from nature – the difference being that for the Christian there is also alienation from God, which for Marx as an atheist, made no sense.

We should note, in passing, how much Marx's view of history has its roots in Plato. The dialectic for Plato was essentially a matter of rational argument, moving from thesis to antithesis to synthesis, as we saw in chapter 3.

G.W.F. Hegel revisited this dialectical process, made it the means by which world history moved and saw behind this movement the workings of a *World Spirit*. Marx, in turn, took this process and (in his words) "turned Hegel on its head", accepting the truth of a dialectical movement in history and not just in rational argument, but making it essentially a matter of material and economic change. Human history was destined to pass from "primitive communism" to a "classical slavery" (which negated primitive communism), to "feudalism", to the rise of capitalism and the bourgeoisie, and then eventually (via the dictatorship of the proletariat) to true communism.

Marx argued that alienation reaches ever greater levels as we pass through the dialectical process, until being finally overcome in true communism. It makes for an interesting contrast with the Christian belief in "original sin", especially in its Greek Orthodox form of an individual and collective moral *weakness*. If it is true that there is a kind of moral weakness in human beings (and therefore an element of truth in the doctrine of original sin), then Marx's idea that, after the revolution, both state and law could wither away is a mistake. Even though *some* alienation, and similarly much human nastiness, is the result of our economic and political systems, this is not true of all of it. Even if we were able to achieve an ideal society (whatever exactly that would be like), human weaknesses and imperfections would lead – I suggest – to the absolute need for some kind of political order.

Given the failure of Marx's predictions concerning revolutions in capitalist countries, most philosophers who find inspiration in the works of Marx have attempted various modifications of his philosophy, and hence we find that there are many serious philosophers who have tried to produce their own "Neo-Marxist" variations on his philosophy. I shall mention just one here, the German-American philosopher Herbert Marcuse (1898-1979). In his works we find an incisive analysis, part historical, part philosophical, of the shortcomings of contemporary forms of capitalism, and its various forms of oppression and alienation. As the title of one his best-known works (*One-Dimensional Man*)[16] suggests, even if we no longer seek a Marxist revolution, we need an adequate critique of the educational, economic, political and social structures under which we live, and which systematically limit the number of dimensions in which we can live.

In the case of every serious philosophical movement, I have suggested that they say something important even if we reject some of their central theses. In the case of Marxism and Neo-Marxism, I suggest that one benefit is the realization of how important it is, when reviewing ethical concerns, to consider *structural* as well as individual problems. For example, if we are to deal adequately with poverty, the solution is not one that simply gives money to the poorest; it is one in which the very structure of our economic and political systems enables all people to achieve at least a minimum level of prosperity and personal dignity.

7. Existentialist theories

It is hard to pinpoint when existentialist philosophy begins because it represents a trend that began in some 19th century

---

[16] Herbert Marcuse, *One-Dimensional Man* (1964: 2nd ed. London: Routledge, 1991).

writers, such as Kierkegaard[17]. It emerges as a full-blown philosophy in the middle of the 20th century, notably with the French philosopher Jean-Paul Sartre (1905-1980). His position I shall outline here – with the warning that other existentialists often held very different views on some topics.

There is, as a starting point, a somewhat technical point to be made, in order to explain what existentialism means, and why Sartre and others place *existence* before *essence*. For the Greeks, human beings (and other animals) have an essential nature, or essence, that is not of their choosing, but which defines what they are truly like, especially when they are flourishing. For Socrates, our mission or essence is to become the kind of intellectual being that knows itself and seeks true knowledge. For Aristotle, it is to accept our role as rational beings, within the great chain of being, and develop the appropriate virtues. He also argued that our true natures are revealed in what we may become.[18] Many subsequent philosophers made similar assumptions about an essence or essential nature. For example, according to Aquinas, our true nature or "end" (*telos*) is to discover that we are made in the image of God, and can only find

---

[17] Soren Kierkegaard (1813-1855) was a Danish philosopher and theologian. He described his life as passing through three phases: an "illusory", "aesthetic" childhood freedom, followed by a conversion to "morality", followed by a conversion to Christianity and the standpoint of faith – in which, he claimed, he had overcome illusion. These changes were not, crucially, the consequences of any rational process, but of an existential free choice, adopting a "higher" level of being. One of the consequences of this standpoint is that ethics is no longer seen as the highest "good", so that the traditional link (for example, in Aquinas, but rooted in Plato), between God and Good, is broken. According to Kierkegaard, for the sake of religion, the "knight of faith" may be called upon to suspend ethical obligations. This has led to major controversy in both philosophy and theology.

[18] Aristotle, *Politics*, 1252b. "The nature of things consists in their end or consummation; for what each thing is when its growth is completed we call the nature of that thing."

our true fulfilment in union with him. For Marx, it was to discover our true natures as "species-beings" and to live accordingly. Other philosophers, such as Hume, did not employ the concept of "essence", but did not formally attack it in the manner of Sartre.

Sartre claimed that accepting any notion of a given essence was to deny an essential freedom to choose to be the kind of person we wanted to be. Hence, for existentialists, *existence* takes priority over any essence. Here, "existence refers to the actual, living experience of the present moment, unshackled by bonds of any kind, including being bound to an essence that we need to discover and conform to". The secret of life (or of Socrates' "the examined life") is to live with a kind of human "authenticity" – a key concept for many existentialists. Absolute freedom to choose not only how to act, but what kind of person we will be, is the mark of what life ought to be about – even if this does not entail happiness.

Sartre wrote a somewhat impenetrable philosophy book (*Being and Nothingness*)[19], but for the most part he spread his philosophy through the medium of novels, in which heroes and antiheroes live out lives of authenticity or (more often) inauthenticity. Here, yet again, we see a link with some other philosophers, remembering that Plato used story and myth to bring to people's attention some of his ideas that a simple description would be unlikely to convey. One recurrent theme in Sartre's novels is what he calls "bad faith" (*mauvaise foi*) as a classic example of "inauthenticity". Many people act out a part, or play a role, that does not express their true nature, because – for the sake of convenience – they choose to live in this more comfortable mode.

On the positive side, there is little doubt that Sartre often makes

---

[19] Jean-Paul Sartre, *Being and Nothingness*. H.E. Barnes tr. (London: Routledge, 1956)

penetrating observations on human life, illuminating actual experience, and exposing certain kinds of pomposity and self-delusion that can rob our lives of fulfilment. Reading his novels often casts a kind of light on what it is actually like to live as human beings in a world where many things seem to be alien and hypocritical. On the negative side, there are at least three substantial problems.

First, Sartre's concept of freedom is neither the freedom to choose to follow the good as we see it (which, of course, involves accepting our "essence") nor is it the kind of freedom that goes with *creative* choice (as when a great artist chooses to draw this picture rather than that, or – I would suggest – an ordinary moral agent chooses this action rather than that, when both are morally legitimate).[20] Instead it is a kind of wild *leap*, which – by its very nature – can have no basis in ethical or aesthetic demands. If it is rooted in a moral or aesthetic demand, then, necessarily, it becomes an acceptance of a kind of essence, of something that binds us in a way that is in tension with Sartre's "authentic living". This is a very puzzling account of freedom, and is linked with the second major problem.

Suppose that my *act* of authenticity is to do something antisocial (say, murder my unpleasant neighbour); does not this then become, for Sartre, a morally good thing to do – that is, if "authenticity" is the key concept in terms of how we ought to act? This possibility has led to much discussion and is linked with the third problem – one that applies to Sartre himself rather than to many of his followers.

---

[20] In theology there has been much discussion (for example, in Augustine) concerning in what sense, if any, God can be said to have freedom (because he necessarily does what is good – at least according to most accounts). One suggestion goes that God has the kind of freedom that goes with the creativity I mention here.

In his later life Sartre combined his existentialist philosophy with an attachment to a form of Marxism. Although this makes it unlikely he would have regarded antisocial behaviour as "authentic", it is highly paradoxical. There is clearly, in Marxism, a significant kind of human essence, namely, to be and to act as "species-beings".

8. Postmodernism

In chapter 7, I suggested a very general definition of the "modern" era. When philosophers refer to *modernism*, then insofar as we can highlight general tendencies – such as reliance on scientific reasoning rather than on ecclesiastical authority – this is the kind of intellectual scene that is meant. The term *postmodernism* is similarly somewhat general and vague, but it clearly implies a rejection of a kind of orthodoxy that typified thinking from around 1500 to the end of the Enlightenment period. This includes any claim that there is a scientific, or universal rationality that all of us should accept. However, postmodernism was anything but a return to pre-modern modes of thought. I have heard a critic of postmodernism argue like this: "According to postmodernism there exists no 'meta-narrative' by which we could or should judge what is right or wrong, true or false, beautiful or ugly; the whole enterprise of traditional philosophy, and even of traditional science, which was to discover universal norms or truths, is fundamentally mistaken. We all see everything from our own, and highly prejudiced standpoints." Following this description of postmodernism, he went on: "The fallacy in postmodernism is obvious. To say 'there is no meta-narrative' is to make a truth claim, and since there are no truth claims (because the very notion of a truth claim is incoherent), in making this claim the postmodernist has refuted himself."

However, this "short cut" argument does not really work, for at least three reasons. First, most postmodernists are too bright to fall, explicitly, into such an obvious fallacy (a fallacy that is a variation on what is called the "self-referential" problem). Second, in order to express the rejection of traditional accounts of truth, instead of making rival truth claims, or providing alternative accounts of rationality, postmodernists tend to use irony – a kind of poetic or indirect reference to their point of view, which avoids describing it in the form of a truth claim. Third, I have suggested in several places in this book that all the great philosophers, however much in error on some matters, make at least one important and useful point: they "lay their fingers" on something that needs to be said. In the case of the postmodernist movement, there is a valuable insight, namely the need to remind ourselves, frequently, that we, like everyone else, see all things from a certain perspective. For example, the categories we use in our language to describe all things already have, implicit within them, certain assumptions about how reality is ordered. Here we may think that postmodernists are actually developing a theme in Kant, and the way in which he stresses how we inevitably structure everything that we contemplate.

I do not myself think that it follows that there cannot be rational grounds for preferring one kind of position to another, but repeatedly, we need to remind ourselves of our prejudices.

Two particularly important postmodernist philosophers, both French, deserve special mention. The first is Jean-Francois Lyotard (1924-1998)[21], and in particular his book *The Postmodern*

---

[21] An important post-humanist French philosopher who attacked central tenets of the Enlightenment, including the supremacy of reason. He argued that the phenomena of reality were so singular that synthesizing theories could not deliver an accurate representation of that reality. He also emphasized the importance of the non-rational and undermined the idea that Western society is characterized by inevitable progress.

Condition (1979)[22]. The second is Michel Foucault (1926-1984)[23]. Although Foucault disclaims the title of "philosopher" his writings are a combination of philosophical, historical, psychological and sociological enquiry. They are always concerned with how power relationships are at work, shaping how, in different contexts, people come to understand themselves. One of his major works is *Madness and Unreason* (with an abridged version titled *Madness and Civilization*)[24].

The study of what counts as "madness" makes an interesting link with the work of Plato, who argued that there are four kinds of divine madness – as well as (by implication) – a fifth type, namely non-divine madness, as when a person is deranged in the normal sense of that term. The four kinds of divine madness, as described in the dialogue called the *Phaedrus*, comprise: (i) insight or prophecy – the gift of Apollo; (ii) the experience of mystic union – the gift of Dionysius; (iii) poetry and the other arts – the gift of the Muses; and (iv) love (*eros*) – the gift of Aphrodite. In all of these, human beings are – as it were – transported out of their ordinary selves into another realm of being. The link (I suggest) with Foucault, is that instead of a kind of *pathology* of madness, there is a serious attempt to understand its many forms and the way in which it is, and has been, connected with power relationships in our society. Here is an extract from Foucault's introduction to the book on madness: "In the serene world of mental illness, modern man no longer communicates with

---

[22] Jean-Francois Lyotard, *The Postmodern Condition*. G. Bennington and B. Massumi, tr. (Manchester: Manchester University Press, 1984)

[23] A French post-humanist whose work can be divided into distinct phases, but who is chiefly referred to in discussions of the nature of power and its expression in institutions, discourse and other forms.

[24] Michel Foucault, *Madness and Civilization* (2nd ed. London: Routledge, 2001). The unabridged text was published by Routledge as *History of Madness* in 2006.

the madman: on the one hand, the man of reason delegates the physician to madness, thereby authorizing a relation only through the abstract universality of disease; on the other, the man of madness communicates with society only by the intermediary of an equally abstract reason which is order, physical and moral constraint, the anonymous pressure of the group, the requirements of conformity."[25]

9. Nihilism

The term nihilism derives from the Latin word for "nothing" (*nihil*), and in philosophy it was originally applied to the thought of a number of Russian anarchist writers of the mid-19th century. Later, the term lost this anarchist emphasis (especially in the context of the Russian anarchists' violent attacks on the political establishment) and came to stand either for a rejection of the rationality of any moral norms, or the claim that all human aspirations were trivial, or for a denial that human life is endowed with any significant meaning (or some mixture of these three claims). Nietzsche is sometimes classed as a nihilist, but the attribution – in my view – is misleading. For example, although he certainly denied the possibility of providing a rational defence of moral norms, he clearly dismissed as wrong-headed some moral ideals (such as Christian concerns for the poor and needy – which he likened to a "slave" morality) and – as we have seen – sought to promote the power and prestige of the *ubermensch*.

10. Conclusion

As indicated, these nine styles of philosophy only represent some of the more influential trends in Western philosophy since 1900. For example, there could also have been sections on *prescriptivism*

---

[25] Translation by Richard Howard, 1967.

(with special reference to Richard Hare)[26]; on contemporary human rights philosophers (with special reference to Alan Gewirth)[27]; on *amoralism* (with special reference to Joel Marks)[28]; on *projectivism* (with special reference to Simon Blackburn)[29]; *absurdism*, with special reference to Albert Camus and Franz Kafka[30] and on recent supporters of a conservative Roman Catholic interpretation of natural law (with special reference to John Finnis)[31].

Question

Does the bewildering array of moral philosophies, proposed by intelligent and well-intentioned thinkers, indicate that there is no possibility of discovering a "correct" version of moral philosophy?

Comment

Perhaps, instead of seeking a single, "correct" moral philosophy, we should be content with finding: (i) one that can – in our view – stand up to rational criticism – for example, in terms of consistency and coherence, and (ii) one that represents a philosophy that – although not the only rational candidate – we find attractive, and (iii)

---

[26] R.M. Hare, "Prescriptivism", in E. Craig ed. *The Routledge Encyclopedia of Philosophy* (London: Routledge, 1998), pp. 19-27

[27] Alan Gewirth, *Human Rights* (Chicago: Chicago University Press, 1982)

[28] Joel Marks, *Ethics without Morals* (London: Routledge, 2012)

[29] Simon Blackburn, *Essays in Quasi-Realism* (New York: Oxford University Press, 1993)

[30] Albert Camus (1913-1960) was a French/Algerian philosopher and novelist, author of *The Outsider* (tr. Sandra Smith, London: Penguin, 2013). Franz Kafka, 1883-1924 was a Czech philosopher/novelist, and author of *The Castle* (tr. W and E Muir, London: Penguin, 1957). In both cases the role of the concept of "truth" can be misunderstood, since, despite the rejection of conventional views, the importance of a kind of integrity is implicit.

[31] John Finnis, *Natural Law and Natural Rights* (2nd ed. Oxford: Oxford University Press, 2011)

one that we think we can actually take on board as a guide to how we should live.

Chapter 12. Some conclusions. The fundamental and abiding questions of moral philosophy

1. Abiding issues

While discussing the ethics of the emotivist, Charles Stevenson, the point was made that whatever the details of our personal moral philosophy (if we have one at all), it must allow for the reality of disagreement. I don't mean the kind of disagreement that occurs when an outside observer can see that one person is clearly right and the other wrong – as in the 15th century dispute concerning whether the earth went round the sun or the sun went round the earth. I mean the kind of disagreement that occurs when equally well-informed, intelligent, and well-meaning persons disagree. Moreover, since there are no easily discoverable "facts" that might settle typical cases of moral disagreement, it is likely that some disagreements will continue.

Let us consider a couple of issues – in the area of moral philosophy – where such disagreement is *unlikely*, and there is a general consensus. First, moral language is not neutral, so that if someone says: "helping the poor is good", then the notion that at least some people (those with the capacity and opportunity) *ought* to do something about it is already implicit within the language used. Similarly, it makes no sense to ask: "Why ought I to do the right thing?" because English at least has evolved to use words such as "ought" and "right" with this implication that we ought to do what is good – as it were – written into their meanings. When Stevenson wrote about the "magnetism" that is attached to many ethical terms, he was making a point that almost all would now acknowledge. Second, when Socrates posed the question: "What is the good life?" he was asking a question that all, or nearly all philosophers will recognize as asking something significant. Nihilism, perhaps, might be defined as pointing to the few people who reject the significance of this question. The answers to "what is the good life?" vary enormously, but even existentialists have their answer (to live with personal authenticity), and most secular philosophers (who do not think that there is any overall purpose or *telos* regarding human life), still hold that we are better off when we invent or choose purposes of some kind.

This said, let us list six of the central issues where there remain wide disagreement among equally well-informed, intelligent, and well-meaning persons.

2. Ethics and metaphysics

With the exception of some of the Sophists, for the Greeks, ethical questions were also metaphysical questions. They were questions about what could be called fundamental truths – such as the true nature of the universe or precisely what God had ordained for human beings. Even if one were an atheist, the notion that some actions or some virtues or some states of affairs were *intrinsically* better than others was one that made sense. This was basically true for most subsequent philosophers until we come to the time of Hume, when both the fundamental meaning and usefulness of traditional metaphysics is called into question. The principal reason for this change of heart – one of the consequences of the Enlightenment –

is that there is no way in which scientific methodologies can give definitive answers to metaphysical questions; and if science is the key to rationality, then traditional metaphysics is either empty of meaning, or – at best – a kind of poetry.

The argument has moved on, in part because of a realization, by many secular philosophers, that abandoning religion does not necessarily mean abandoning metaphysics. All kinds of foundational questions, for example, about the nature of scientific methodology, remain. These questions may not be solvable by empirical methods, but it is also widely recognized that there may be other rational criteria, such as consistency, comprehensiveness and fruitfulness that apply. For example, in literary criticism, there is no empirical way of proving that novel A is a great novel, while novel B is relatively trash, but the manner in which critics argue has many rational components, including the three just listed. A great novel, for example, may be said to illuminate the human condition by the way which the characters are described. Clearly, as this example shows, rationality should not be limited to the empirical and mathematical methods of inquiry.

The result is that some contemporary philosophers (including moral realists, and at least some supporters of human rights), either explicitly or implicitly, use metaphysical notions as part of their approach to moral philosophy, while others (including many emotivists) do not. If we say that all human beings have an intrinsic human dignity, or have certain basic human rights, then this can reasonably be taken to mean that these rights have some basis in the way that everyone ought to view the world. If this basis is purely a matter of psychology – insisting that this is how we are likely to feel – it is not clear that this captures the force of what is being claimed, namely that all people ought to feel this way. Thus, it may be argued, some claim about the ultimately proper way of seeing rights is being suggested, and this – in turn – at least invites metaphysical language about what is ultimately true or real.

Nevertheless, one of the abiding questions in moral philosophy is simply this: In what sense, if any, are metaphysical issues important for moral philosophy?

3. Objectivity and subjectivity

The issue of whether moral actions and virtues have an objective or a subjective status overlaps issues relating to metaphysics. However, in this case, the fundamental issues are even more mired in ambiguity than the question of the importance of metaphysics.

Serious discussions of ethical issues are certainly "objective" in at least two senses.[1] First, one of the ways in which we use the term is simply to say that the speaker is not showing manifest bias. A position is being proposed "objectively" because the proposer's opinion is not influenced by his or own interest. For instance, he or she is not being paid to present a certain position, regardless of its merit. Here we may recall Socrates' disdain for rhetoric when not in the service of truth. Second, the word "objective" can refer to the fact that the position being proposed is backed up by some reasons, rather than simply being asserted as a matter of feeling. If someone were to say: "Hunting is wrong because I don't like it, rather as I happen not to like tomato soup", we would not be impressed, because while matters of taste (such as one's liking or disliking tomato soup) are generally held to be merely matters of personal preference, moral statements (such as "hunting is wrong") are generally held to be

---

[1] Readers who have understood – as a result of critical thinking – how careful we have to be with the use of words, will notice how I have made an assumption here, because by using the word "serious" I may have already implied the two criteria that I name.

opinions for which one can be expected to offer some kind of reason or argument. For example, the person expressing such a view would normally be able to add something like "because it causes pain to animals". Similarly, the person who disagrees would normally be able to offer reasons of a kind, such as "hunting is, in my view, the best way of culling animals that need to be culled." On this issue my concern is not to argue who is right and who is wrong, but simply to point out that in all ordinary cases, there is a kind of objectivity on both sides of the argument, simply because both give reasons that (i) seem good to them (in contrast with any mere expression of feeling), and (ii) might reasonably be expected to carry some weight with the person they are disagreeing with.

However, once anyone claims that morality is objective in some other way, perhaps because – it is alleged – it is the proper conclusion of a utilitarian measurement, or a Kantian application of the categorical imperative, then we enter huge disagreement. Perhaps we might agree that it is misleading to refer to moral facts – as some moral realists do – but if we are still happy to talk about moral "truths" then this is the language of some, but certainly not all moral philosophers. Few within either the emotivist or existentialist schools of thought would want to think of moral objectivity in this way.

4. Ethics and religion

Let me summarize the position I have defended in this book. Ethics is an inquiry into what is good and bad, right or wrong, virtuous and vicious. Meta-ethics discusses the theories according to which we may be able to think about what is right and wrong, in general; practical ethics is its application to specific issues, such as whether or not states should practise capital punishment. For some, there is a rational aspect to ethics; for almost all, ethical enquiry is also intimately related to human passions and emotions, in addition to certain kinds of reason that have been put forward in argument. Religion, in contrast – I have suggested – is a human response to certain "non-rational" experiences (that are neither, in themselves, rational nor irrational); and moreover, in typical cases, the response is in some ways collective, so that there are shared notions of what is sacred.[2] Three such kinds of experience (among others) can be described as: (i) Both individual and collective experiences of being caught up in some community "whole" that is greater than oneself (for example, a collective sense of solidarity that accompanies the performance of some rituals).[3] (ii) A sense of awe or ultimate unity or of being in the presence of a greater whole or (for some people) a sense of being in the presence of a love that transcends our understanding. In one sense, at least, these experiences are real in that they refer to types of psychological experience that have been subject to studies – sometimes under the heading of mysticism. Disagreement arises when we ask whether – in additional to being psychological experiences – they can also be intimations of another level of reality. (iii) The sense of a call or vocation to follow a

---

[2] The philosopher and theologian John Hick has argued that all the great religions are (in their own ways) responses to an awareness of the same ultimate reality. See especially his *The Fifth Dimension* (London: Oneworld, 1999). We should note that although he supports what is sometimes called religious pluralism, this is not the same as saying that all religions are really the same, which is the contention of Aldous Huxley in his *The Perennial Philosophy* (London: Chatto and Windus, 1946) – because the "awareness" can be and is interpreted in different ways. For example, there is genuine disagreement concerning whether individual persons are of ultimate significance (as in mainstream Christianity), or whether they are ultimately illusory (as in Theravada Buddhism). The former – when using a metaphor for the ultimate significance of the individual – is likely to prefer that of a piece of stone within a great mosaic (where the individual has a lasting importance within the great scheme of things), the latter, that of a drop of water being absorbed into a great ocean.

[3] For Emile Durkheim, this was the central feature of religion.

certain way of life, to join a religious organization and/or to follow a particular leader. All three of these contexts may impact on how we view what "ought" to be done, and therefore have an impact on ethics, but they are not themselves simply ethical. I hold therefore, that we should not confuse religion with ethics, but – as I have suggested – claim that religion can be a force, either for good (as in the attack on the slave trade, from the days of John Woolman,[4] or the early days of the hospice movement) or for evil (as in the history of religious persecution).[5] Whether or not there is religious truth, separate from moral truth, is another example of an issue on which philosophers disagree.

5. Human rights

The notion of individual human rights did not enter the arena of moral philosophy until the 1600s, even though the notion of "right" (as in the Latin *ius*) is much older. One view is that the concept was introduced by some of the Levellers (a group of political activists, driven by an individualistic version of Protestantism), in England around 1640. Although, at this time, these alleged rights were seen as being granted by God, an emphasis on human rights was soon taken up by writers who were essentially or principally secular. Perhaps the most famous of these is Thomas Paine, whose *Rights of Man* was first published in 1791. Human rights, by then, formed a hallmark of political radicalism, notably in the rhetoric of the French Revolution of 1789 and the American War of Independence. However, the "inalienable rights" asserted in the American Declaration of

---

[4] John Woolman (1720-1772) was the American Quaker who, in the 1740s, initiated the anti-slavery movement on the grounds of its incompatibility with Christianity.

[5] There is an ancient Latin phrase *corruptio optimi pessima*, meaning "the corruption of the best is the worst", and this can convey the idea that if religion can be a force for the best, bad religion could be expected to be a particularly bad form of evil.

Independence (1776) claims these rights as an endowment from God. J.S. Mill, the secular moral philosopher discussed in chapter 9, was anxious to find a place for human rights within his overall utilitarianism.[6] Among other seminal works we should also mention Mary Wollstonecraft's *A Vindication of the Rights of Woman* (1792).

While discussions of human rights form a significant element in both moral philosophy and international law, there are – at the same time – a number of highly disputed philosophical issues that relate to them. For example: (i) how exactly should human rights be defined? Do they, for example, depend on some kind of "meta-narrative" of the kind that is anathema to postmodernists?; (ii) What exactly is the scope of human rights? Do they, for example, guarantee a minimum level of education, or wealth, or of opportunities for employment to all people?; (iii) Do human rights apply equally to all persons (including the very young, the very disabled, the very demented, those in prison)?; (iv) Do the same rights, or analogous rights, apply to non-human animals, and if so, how do we balance them with human rights? (For example, are we justified in destroying the habitat of tigers, in order for local human beings to flourish, to the extent that tigers become extinct?) Issues such as these provide another area where moral philosophy is very much an ongoing activity.

6. Rationality and ethics

We have seen that for Kant, moral philosophy is basically a rational exercise, rooted in his arguments concerning the good will (as the only truly intrinsic good) and the categorical imperative – which

---

[6] Although, if one is a utilitarian, human rights cannot form the foundation for a moral philosophy, (because this basis is provided by "the greatest happiness" principle). Mill argued that a settled emphasis on human rights, in both the thinking and the legislation of all countries, is likely to increase overall happiness.

involves an exercise in practical reason. In contrast, we find Hume arguing that reason is, and ought to be, the slave of the passions. Almost all philosophers (nihilists being an exception) allow some role for reason – including Hume – but how extensive that role is, and in what manner it ought to be employed, continue to be matters on which there is strong disagreement.

The issue of the relevance of rationality to moral philosophy is complicated by the fact that although almost all of us use the terms "reason" and "rationality", and hold that these are "good" things, there is considerable disagreement about exactly how to define the rational. My own view is that we should begin by distinguishing procedural rationality from substantive rationality. The former is easier to describe and includes concepts such as *audi alteram partem* – Latin for "listen to the other side (of the argument)". Even in a high school essay, when an argument is put forward for a certain point of view, a rational presentation lays out the most likely objection, and then responds to it. There are other procedural considerations, such as "consider what ambiguities are implicit in the language used". Another is whether logic and the kind of critical thinking explored in this book have been used whenever they are appropriate. Much harder to resolve is how to evaluate claims concerning a substantive rationality – namely that position x is the rational position to hold. Even in a discipline such as physics, there can be serious disagreement concerning fundamental theories, each of which is backed by rational considerations. Even more clearly, moral philosophers continue to disagree not only about which moral theory, if any, to adopt, but concerning which is the most rational in the light of our overall experience of life. We can agree to use terms such as coherence, comprehension and fruitfulness, but all of these terms require more analysis than is often realized.

Further clarification of the terms "reason" and "rationality" can be provided by noting a distinction between two aspects of how these terms are used. The first is sometimes referred to as "discursive reason", and proceeds in a step-by-step manner through a logical sequence; it marks a process or procedure. The steps in a typical mathematical proof are an example (ending "QED", for the Latin *quod erat demonstrandum* – "which was [the matter] to be proved"). The second is a kind of "insight" that arises, often suddenly and spontaneously, when a pattern is recognized. A typical example is when an apparently random set of dots is seen as a picture. Similarly, all teachers know how pupils suddenly "see" or "recognize" a point that has been made. The Latin words *ratio* and *intellectus* sometimes mark these two aspects of rationality.[7]

7. Western values

This is a book about moral philosophy in the Western world – while admitting that that there is a fuzzy line between what counts as Western and Eastern. However, one of the issues in moral philosophy is exactly how far moral values are, or ought to be, universal – applicable to all human beings as human beings, regardless of the cultures in which they are born and raised.

As soon as this question is asked, one of the issues that arise concerns the claim that, historically, many Western values do not represent good candidates for a universal ethic, because they demonstrate colonial or imperial ambitions, dressed up and made to look respectable by a claim that they represent true, universal values. Consider the attempts to justify the Crusades against the Muslim world, beginning in

---

[7] On the distinction between *ratio* and *intellectus* see Michael J. Langford, "Pre-Modern Interfaith Dialogues with Special Reference to Nicholas of Cusa" in *The Medieval History Journal* Vol.20 (2017), pp. 118-147.

1096; or the many anti-Jewish pogroms; or the Spanish and Portuguese conquests in South America (by the *conquistadores*), starting in the late 1400s; or the treatment of aboriginal people in the U.S., Canada and Australia; or the British Opium Wars of the mid-19th century in China; and many more colonial or imperial acts of violence. Clever people have attempted to find moral arguments in favour of all these dreadful episodes. This is despite the fact these arguments would be rejected by all the theories we have described, with the possible exceptions of nihilism and amoralism, on the grounds that there are no rational considerations that apply.

An awareness of this colonial and imperial past has led many moral philosophers to be wary of claiming the superiority of Western values – as if they always represent the discovery of genuinely universal values. If we observe Western practice, philosophers have frequently failed to be sufficiently critical of evil practices. The situation is complicated because if we look carefully we do find cases where brave philosophers have criticized their own countries and their own cultures for what they have been doing. For example, in the Middle Ages, Abelard criticized his Church for the way it persecuted heretics. In the 1500s, Francisco Vitoria criticized his country for the enslavement of indigenous South Americans, and there are many other examples. Nevertheless, these brave people were the exception rather than the norm.

Perhaps one of the conclusions we should draw is this. When we ask what the best system is for a people, if they are to survive and to flourish, the answer has to include an awareness of, and sensitivity to, the history and culture of that particular people. There may be universal values of a very general kind (such as that expressed in the Golden Rule); however, the way in which these values should be substantiated in any particular country cannot easily be discovered simply by asking universal questions – abstracted from the local conditions. Take the example of the monarchy. The United Kingdom has a constitutional monarchy, which – especially since the Revolution of 1688-1689 – has strictly limited powers. If I had time and space I could proceed to give a defence of this system, *for the U.K.*, taking into account its history; its culture; the way in which – for the most part – it seems to work; the dangers that accompany constitutional change; the problems associated with alternatives;[8] and so on. However, even if I am right, in no way does it follow that, say, France or Ireland, given their histories and cultures, should start to have constitutional monarchies. Given their histories and cultures, these countries are better served by other constitutional forms.

One consequence of this awareness is extreme caution in applying typical Western values to (say) the political and constitutional systems in Asia – at least without a thorough knowledge and appreciation of the complex histories and cultures that are to be found there. If, even in Europe, there can be such legitimate variation with respect to forms of government, how much more is this likely to be the case globally. I am not saying that there are no lessons to be learned, and no universal values to uphold, but the history of colonialism and imperialism makes me very nervous about asserting what these lessons should be.

---

[8] There are grounds for wanting to divide the positions of chief executive (in the U.K. this is the Prime Minister) from the head of state (the Queen). (For example, such a division tends to lessen cults of personality, in which single individuals have too much power and prestige.) In the U.K., if the head of state were to be elected by the whole population, this would – at least psychologically – give them a degree of authority that the present monarch does not have, thus changing the balance of power. If the head of state were appointed, or elected by parliament, there would be the real and present danger of appointing some political hack. (This was one of the concerns that led Australian voters to reject a proposal to abandon the monarchy.)

8. Towards a possible overall moral philosophy

In this final section I am going to take a risk, and suggest my own response to the situation that moral philosophy finds itself in at this time. My response is a kind of dialectic involving three steps.

(i) The Hartian origin of moral language

We need to distinguish the historical and psychological origins of moral language and moral sentiments from issues concerning what sense we make of them when we stand back and reflect on our moral language and moral sentiments. A similar point was made by the American philosopher and psychologist William James (1842-1910). In his seminal book *The Varieties of Religious Experience* (1902), James warns the reader about confusing the question of how we explain or understand the *origins* of beliefs or practices with the question of how we should understand or interpret these things now. Sometimes philosophers use the term "the genetic fallacy" or "the fallacy of origins" to describe this danger. To take a crude example, if a theologian claimed the sun was the centre of the solar system, and not the earth, simply because of an interpretation of a passage in the Bible, this (non-rational, or even irrational, origin for belief) would not falsify the claim!

In my view, the most plausible account of how moral language – along with its "magnetic" power – *originated*, is that given by the Oxford philosopher and jurist, H.L.A. (Herbert) Hart (1907-1992), especially in his book *The Concept of Law* (1961).[9] The key

---

[9] It so happens that Herbert Hart was my first tutor in philosophy, at New College, Oxford, in 1951 – just before he was made professor of jurisprudence. Subsequently, I was fortunate to be tutored by both Isaiah Berlin and Stuart Hampshire. My support for Hart's general position does not imply acceptance of the whole theory expounded in *The Concept of Law*. For example, his exposition of what he calls "the rule of recognition" raises many problems.

concept is that of a "social rule", which helps to bind communities together. Such a rule is present, Hart argues, not simply when there is convergent action, but when the rule has an "interior aspect", so that most people regard the presence of the rule as a reason for acting in a certain way. When the rule is violated, most people feel a sense of shame or guilt or remorse. However, these feelings are not the principal indication of a social rule. Hart argues: "When they [individuals] say they 'feel bound' to behave in certain ways" they may refer to certain feelings, but these feelings are neither necessary nor sufficient for "the existence of 'binding' rules" ... "What is necessary is that there should be a critical reflective attitude to certain patterns of behaviour as a common standard ...".[10]

It is not difficult to provide what I would call a quasi-Darwinian account of how and why such rules arise. One of Hart's suggestions for a universal moral rule – part of what he calls a "minimum content" version of the old natural law – is one that restricts violence within the community of which one is part. A community that does not have this rule will simply lose out to those communities that do, perhaps in terms of the efficiency of their hunting enterprises or defensive wars or the sheer struggle to cope with a hostile environment. Moreover, unless there is internalization the moral rule will not be consistently kept, except when others are watching. However, it is simply impractical to rely on a host of external police, and – when there is the psychological possibility of a sort of internal police officer – unnecessary. Further again, it is not essential that every single individual has this internal police officer; it just has to be so common that the social systems function most of the time. Those that do not share the internalization will tend to become social

---

[10] H.L.A. Hart, *The Concept of Law* (Oxford: Clarendon Press, 1961), p. 56

outcastes. It may be possible for a small minority to live within the society *as if* they had such an internal attitude, while in practice they play a kind of long-term charade – a situation that reminds me of the "free rider" problem in Hobbes.

When did these social rules emerge? Probably in the early days of *Homo sapiens*, indeed as soon as communal life, combined with primitive language, began. Very likely they were also found in other species of *homo*, and perhaps – in some degree – in primates.[11] One of the important consequences of this approach, for moral philosophy, is that the notion of moral *obligation* – that is of a sense of being bound by a rule, is perfectly explainable without introducing further considerations. It suggests, for example, that the Cambridge philosopher Elizabeth Anscombe was wrong to insist that moral obligation only made sense if it reflected the demands of a personal God (in her influential paper "Modern Moral Philosophy").[12] This is another example of my theme that philosophy and religion need to be separated, although they can influence each other.

Suppose someone asks: "Where does a sense of moral obligation come from, if it does not reflect either the command of a God or of some privately felt passion – say, to offer help and sympathy to others?" It is important to understand the subtle answer that a Hartian position suggests. Social rules are not only psychological phenomena (rooted in the kind of social beings that we are), they also exhibit what might be called a certain "grammar" or internal logic. One obvious example is that if an action is held to be good, then

---

[11] I recently heard an account, by a primatologist, of the reaction by a group of chimpanzees to an act of infanticide by a rogue male. The widespread expression of outrage and horror suggested that some kind of social rule had been violated.

[12] From *Philosophy*. Vol. 33 (1958). pp. 1-19 reprinted in G.E.M. Anscombe, *Philosophical Papers*. Vol. 3 (Oxford: Blackwell, 1981).

this, in itself, provides a reason for doing it. This implication is part of the grammar or structure of moral language as it develops; there does not need to be some kind of extra-linguistic reason for opting for the good, outside the structure of moral discourse (even though there might be one). Thus a sense of moral obligation (leading to the appropriate use of words such as "ought" and "should") is written into the structure of how moral language develops. It is also true, of course, that this sense of obligation (a kind of internal bond), could only arise because of our biological and psychological natures, which – unlike machines – have drives and pressures within them, such as care for our young. To put this another way: once we properly understand the nature of a social rule, a sense of moral obligation "goes with the territory".

(ii) The impact of "the reflective turn"

Hart's account of the origin of social rules is in part psychology and in part biology, because the rules depend on certain human capacities and vulnerabilities – for example, the fact that we can be in mortal danger while we sleep. However, my contention is that once we have critical thinking, the mere presence of these social rules becomes the focus of a new kind of intellectual curiosity. Prior to what I call "the reflective turn" (in its early days, typified by, though not necessarily limited to, Greek philosophy of the classical period), a question like: "Is this social rule – say about incest – a good rule?" not only could not be answered, it could not easily have been asked! The very idea that a social rule, which provided one with moral language and moral categories (such as actions that were right or wrong), could itself be the subject of intellectual examination, would have been bizarre, and – I suggest – unintelligible to most ancient people.[13]

To put this in another way: in its early stages, the raw material for moral *philosophy* was the awareness of a set of social rules, some of which were absolutely necessary for the very maintenance of social living. Once these rules become themselves the object of critical thinking, a totally new situation emerged, because prior to this reflective turn, any appeal to morality was precisely an appeal to these same social rules that are now being examined.

(iii) The agape revolution

The reflective turn, emerging in the Greek culture around 500-300 BCE, and – in slightly different forms – in some other regions of the world during the Axial Age, does not mark the end of the dialectic. The emergence of the concept of love (Greek *agape*), produces another phase in the way moral philosophers have reflected on the human condition. There were several sources for this new emphasis on the kind of love for which the word *agape* came to be used. The emphasis on compassion in Buddhism, and the way of devotion (*bhakti*) within Hinduism, brought to attention analogous ideas. Also, a number of rabbis, prior to the ministry of Jesus, stressed this kind of love in their interpretation of the Hebrew Scriptures – stressing, for example, the "loving kindness" of God in the *Book of Hosea*.[14] The actual word *agape* was introduced into Greek culture, in part at least, because this word was used in the Greek translation

---

[13] Perhaps there would be some analogy in a situation where a religious prophet proposed a radical change in the way sacrifices, were to be carried out. This seems to have happened in ancient Israel when human sacrifice was replaced by animal sacrifice.

[14] The *Septuagint* often used the Greek word *agape* for love, but in the case of the "lovingkindness" of God in *Hosea* (Hebrew *hesed*) the actual Greek word used is the one for mercy.

Some conclusions

of the Hebrew Bible known as the *Septuagint*,[15] which circulated widely after about 200 BCE.

Plato had two principal words for "love": *eros*, which, for him, included more than sexual attraction; and *philia*, that can roughly be translated as "friendship". Although it would be absurd to say that love, in the sense of *agape*, did not exist before the spread of the Christian gospels in the first century CE, their impact, and of the other traditions just mentioned, caused a revolution in how moral philosophy evolved. For example, Jesus' demand that we should even love our enemies was truly revolutionary. Here, in this new emphasis on *agape*, was a kind of "good" that seemed to transcend earlier accounts of what human relationships could be like and to which they should aspire.

Love (*agape*) is one of those concepts which is often best described indirectly, through stories such as Jesus' parable of the Good Samaritan; but more succinct pointers to its meaning can be given which help to show how it overlaps with concepts such as forgiveness, mercy, grace, trust and fidelity. The American philosopher Martha Nussbaum describes it as including "a delighted recognition of the other as valuable, special and fascinating".[16] Another pointer can be found in the notion of paying *attention*, a connection powerfully brought out in the work of the English philosopher and novelist, Iris Murdoch. Attention is "a just and loving gaze directed upon an individual reality".[17] This attention can be directed to an object in nature that makes the inherent beauty of

---

[15] The word "Septuagint" (from the Latin for seventy) was used for the Greek text of the Old Testament because of a tradition that the Hebrew original had been translated by seventy scholars.

[16] Martha Nussbaum, *Political Emotions* (Cambridge, Mass: Belknap Press, 2013), p. 176.

[17] Iris Murdoch, *The Sovereignty of Good* (London: Routledge and Kegan Paul, 1970), p. 34, quoting Simone Weil.

creation more apparent to the observer, but here I am more concerned with attention paid to a particular person – a kind of focusing. It is the opposite of the casual handshake at a party in which one is only too aware that the other is looking past you, waiting to meet someone of real importance![18] The uniqueness or particularity of the person who is loved, as well as their preciousness, is central to this understanding of love – one that I once heard described as "bearing witness to persons in all their complexities".

This emphasis on the value of the individual person leads Martha Nussbaum to advance an interesting criticism of Plato's account of *eros*, and especially of his claim that genuine love always seeks "perfection". Love, she argues, should have three characteristics – compassion, individuality and reciprocity – and her emphasis on individuality, in particular, stresses the way in which love accepts and treasures persons as they are ("warts and all") rather than as not-yet completed manifestations of perfect beauty.[19] If we are to expound the concept of love as taught by the likes of Jesus, I hold that Nussbaum is right, although it could still be conceded that Plato had a genuine insight, namely that in loving an individual we have in our minds both what they are and what they may become – an ideal that we hope to foster in our relationship with them.

If I am right in emphasizing the emergence of this sense of love, and of its overriding importance in human life, then there are major consequences for moral philosophy. The most obvious one is this. Any suggestion that loving our neighbour, with the kind

---

[18] However, the realization that attention can be given to the "beautiful" – in art or nature – and also to the "true", as in the rapt attention of a dedicated scientist or historian when about their work, helps us to appreciate why Plato brought together the good, the true and the beautiful.

[19] For a discussion of this matter see Lillian Wilde, "Embracing Imperfection: Plato vs Nussbaum on Love" in *Philosophy Now*. Vol. 12. (Oct./Nov. 2017), pp. 12-14.

of love now being considered, is the overriding obligation, does not fit comfortably into any *system of ethics*. In the first place, it seems alien to a utilitarianism where we solemnly try to weigh one set of potential pleasures with another. Perhaps such utilitarian considerations ought to be in the minds of politicians when they try to balance the outcomes of different economic options, but it does not seem to fit the work of say, the Quaker and social reformer, Elizabeth Fry, when she felt compelled to devote her life to prison reform, or doctors working for *Médecins Sans Frontières* (some of whom are driven by a sense of religious vocation, but others by a sense of moral obligation rooted in secular humanism). Cool calculation just doesn't capture what is going on here. Kant's categorical imperative might fare a little better, because "treating everyone as ends in themselves" does have some analogy with loving them, but does not capture the attention and loving regard referred to above. Perhaps virtue ethics, insofar as it can be understood as a system, is most easily reconciled with the notion that love is the overriding consideration, because expressing and feeling love can be understood as a special kind of virtue. Nevertheless, I am inclined to think that the very effort to find a fully-fledged "system" of ethics may be a mistake; that is, if by system, we mean an overall account of our moral obligations through which we could always decide what we ought to do. I am thoroughly opposed to the kind of (extreme) relativism that denies that anything is truly right or wrong. However, (as already intimated) I take the view that there are some issues where equally honest, intelligent and well-informed people can legitimately disagree.

The difficulty of capturing the full power of love, especially in its creative aspect, helps to explain the role of the "holy fool" in European Renaissance literature, and the character of Nasrudin in

Sufi (Islamic) literature. Both illustrate how creative goodness cannot be captured by systems.

Perhaps this reflection brings us back to Socrates' claim that "the unexamined life is not worth living". One way or another, if we are intellectually alive, we are all challenged to ask ourselves: "what – if anything – is life really about?" or – if we don't like that way of putting the matter:[20] "what kind of life do we choose to adopt?" If love is felt to be the most valuable thing that we can give and receive, then somehow we have to live with this in mind. It clearly indicates that some courses of action and some character traits are to be avoided, but it is not like a map or blueprint that lays out exactly how and when we should act. "Love proceeds by no assured programme".[21] The moral life is more like an adventure and a challenge than the adoption of a formula. It has something in common with a musical performance of a masterpiece, where – once again – there is no one right way of playing it, but there are certainly wrong ways![22]

All the serious moral philosophies we have examined may have something to teach us – they are like bits and pieces of the distilled wisdom that flow from wise men and women – but none of them can fully capture the sense of Socrates' call to examine how we live.

An emphasis on love as a key, or the key concept in moral philosophy, has an interesting connection with Aristotle. Some

---

[20] Some may object that phrasing the question in this way already assumes some kind of moral realism.

[21] This is how the matter is put by W.H. Vanstone in his powerful account of the nature of love (including its vulnerability and unpredictability) in his *Love's Endeavour, Love's Expense* (London: Darton, Longman and Todd, 2007). p. 46.

[22] Once again, this truth may help us to grasp why Plato linked together not only the good with the true but also with the beautiful.

virtues are only required because we live in a very imperfect world in which there is need for pity and forgiveness and reaching out to those in pain. These, for the most part, are what Aristotle called the "moral" virtues and others have called "civic" virtues. Others, such as courage and temperance, are needed because of our own shortcomings, and we might call these "purgatorial" virtues. But let us suppose that we lived in a perfect world, either on earth or elsewhere, in which there was no suffering, selfish desire, and so forth — would we still need virtues? Aristotle would say "Yes"; we need what he called the "intellectual virtues" that reflect for him, the life lived by the gods, or for us, the ideal life of a perfectly ordered society. If we can envision such an extraordinary world, in order to live as fulfilled persons we would still need a raft of virtues, such as the ability to be open to the wonders and beauties of nature and music. These are the virtues emphasized both by Plotinus and by many other religious writers. Among them, and chief of these, would be a love that treasured all beautiful things, especially other persons. Aristotle himself did not place *agape* at the centre of this ideal kind of life (although he took a step towards it with his emphasis on the value of true friendship), but we have moved, I suggest, to a realization that love, in the sense of *agape*, should be the central theme of any adequate moral philosophy.[23]

The idea of a dialectical movement, within moral philosophy from (i) social rules to (ii) a reflective turn to (iii) an agape revolution, not only has implications concerning the limits to any attempt to *systematize* moral thinking, it also has implications for practical ethics. Let me end by considering one of the best and most ancient formulations for a practical guide on to how to live; a six-

---

[23] Both Aquinas, and Spinoza, for different reasons, placed the love of God as the supreme virtue.

word guide originally found in a Jewish source (*Micah* 6.8) but one that can be used equally by those of any religious faith or none. "Do justice; Love mercy; Walk humbly".

The first injunction, "Do justice" is relatively straightforward. Although it is easy, particularly for philosophers, to come up with difficult scenarios when it is not certain what is the right thing to do, most of the time it is perfectly obvious how we ought to act; that is, to "Do Justice": we must refrain from causing unnecessary pain, or breaking the usual rules of social interaction, except when there is some special reason to do so. This, essentially, is level (i), that of social rules.

The second injunction, "Love mercy", is harder. If we are sensitive we recognize that always obeying the rules, strictly, can lead to more suffering and pain than is necessary. A humane society, in which the vast majority is happier, is one in which there is a place for mercy – for reaching out to those in need (physically or mentally or spiritually), a reaching out that goes beyond the call of strict justice, and that is even, on occasions, in tension with it. Here there is a resonance with the "reflective turn" (level ii) that does not take the established social rules as the sole source of ethics, but seeks to *ponder* how these rules need to be modified in order to establish a more wholesome society.

The third injunction, "Walk humbly", might look simple, but it is the hardest. Consider two extremes, both to be avoided. Example A: a person who walks (both literally and metaphorically) as if he owns the world and is surrounded by lesser mortals; a life characterized by a sense of self-importance and arrogance. Example B: a person who walks (both literally and metaphorically) as if they were of no significance, a mere slave or appendage to more important people.

Person A is not walking humbly, not because they walk upright, and with a sense of well-being and of enjoyment in the beauties that may surround them – both of which are good; but because A sees himself as intrinsically more important than others. However, B's fault is just as great. His is a false humility – rooted in a failure to realize the preciousness of all persons, including himself. We are told to "love our neighbour as ourselves", not more than ourselves. Seeking to achieve this balance – between the joy of realizing one's own worth and the responsibility of respecting the worth of others, is a direct result of the *agape* revolution (level iii), a revolution in which we recognize the intrinsic dignity and value of all human beings. It is not an insight that leads to a formula as to how to live, or a system to which to conform; it is more like the call to a creative adventure.

Suggested further reading

Chapter 1

MacIntyre, Alasdair, *A Short History of Ethics* (London: Routledge, 1966)

Raphael, D.D., *Moral Philosophy* (2nd ed. Oxford: Oxford University Press, 1994)

Chapter 2

Guardini, R. (tr. B. Wrighton), *The Death of Socrates* (London: Sheed and Ward, 1948)

Chapter 3

Renault, Mary, *The Mask of Apollo* (London: Four Square Books, 1967).

A work of fiction that brings many aspects of Plato's thought into focus.

Taylor, A.E., *Plato, the Man and his Work* (new ed. London: Routledge, 2012)

Chapter 4

Lloyd, G.E.R., *Aristotle: The Growth and Structure of his Thought* (Cambridge: Cambridge University Press, 1968)

Chapter 5

Chadwick, Henry, *Early Christian thought and the Classical Tradition: Studies in Justin, Clement, and Origen* (Oxford: Clarendon, 1966)

Chapter 6

Passerin d'Entreves, A. *Natural Law* ([1951] new ed. London: Transaction Publishers, 1994)

Gilson, Etienne, *God and Philosophy* (New Haven: Yale University Press, 1959)

Gilson, Etienne, *The Spirit of Medieval Philosophy* ([1932] University of Notre Dame Press, 1991)

Chapter 7

Warrender, H., *The Political Philosophy of Hobbes* (Oxford: Clarendon, 1957)

Chapter 8

Stewart, J.B., *The Moral and Political Philosophy of David Hume* (New York: Columbia University Press, 1963)

Chapter 9

Plamenatz, John, *The English Utilitarians* (Oxford: Blackwell, 1966)

Chapter 10

Paton, H.J., *The Moral Law* (London: Hutchinson, 1948 and many later editions)

Ward, Keith, *The Development of Kant's View of Ethics* (Oxford: Blackwell, 1972)

Chapter 11

Nussbaum, Martha C., *The Fragility of Goodness* (Cambridge: Cambridge University Press, 1986)

Parfit, Derek, *Reasons and Persons* (Oxford: Clarendon, 1984)

Urmson, J.O., *The Emotive Theory of Ethics* (London: Hutchinson, 1968)

Warnock, Mary, *Ethics since 1900* (3rd ed. Oxford: Oxford University Press, 1978)

Warnock, Mary, *Existentialism* (Oxford: Oxford University Press, 1966)

Chapter 12

Hart, H.L.A., *The Concept of Law* (Oxford: Clarendon, 1961)

Vanstone, W.H., *Love's Endeavour, Love's Expense* (London: Darton, Longman and Todd, 2007)

Index

A

Abelard 91n, 194
Agape vi, 59, 69-70, 76, 200-05, 207
Akrasia (weakness of will) 48,
Alexander the Great 39
Allegory vi, 29, 32, 35, 48
Amoralism 182, 194
Anscombe, Elizabeth 198, 198n
A posteriori vii, 143
A priori 143, 145
Aquinas 55, 71-3, 75, 79-95, 96, 102, 115, 120, 155, 159-62, 175, 175n, 205n
Archimedes 7
Aristotle vi, ix, 8n, 9, 20, 36n, 37n, 39-54, 56, 56n, 60, 66, 81-2, 85, 92, 97, 99, 101, 104, 129, 134, 138, 144, 148-9, 153, 155, 160-2, 164, 175, 175n, 205
Atheism vi, 15, 64n, 91, 99-100, 172n, 185
Athens 12-15, 18, 22, 31, 80
Augustine of Hippo 55, 69-74, 94, 177n
Austin, John L. 169n
Ayer, A.J. 167, 167n, 169

B

Bacon, Francis 143
Baxter, Richard 78
Bede (the Venerable) 127
Bentham, Jeremy 128-36, 163-4
Berkeley, George 143
Berlin, Isaiah 196n
Blackburn, Simon 182, 182n
Bohr, Niels 103n
Bramhall, John 100n
Buddhism 7, 43, 58-9, 64, 64n, 90, 189n, 200

C

Calvin, John 80-1, 81n, 84, 86n, 102, 102n, 116
Camus, Albert 182, 182n
Capra, Fritjof 103n
Categorical imperative 150-1, 154-7, 154n, 188, 191, 203
Catholic vi, x, 79-80, 80n, 90-2, 96, 116, 153, 182
Charles II 113
Chillingworth, William 91n
Christendom 55, 71-2, 85
Christian/Christianity vi, x, 28, 55, 49n, 62-4, 64n, 66-72, 79-82, 85-6, 88, 90-92, 96,105, 110, 117, 127, 172n, 173, 175n, 181, 189n, 190n, 201
Civil Law (ius civile) 6, 71n, 85-8, 93-4, 133
Coke, Edward 111n
Coleridge, Samuel Taylor 136n
Condorcet 117
Confucius/Confucianism 5, 30, 64, 66, 85-6
Conscience 94, 152-3
Constantine 55, 71
Contract (see also covenant) 96, 114

Conventional justice 46, 50-1, 162
Copernicus, Nicolaus 144
Covenant (see also contract) 106, 108
Cowan, Brian 117n
Critical thinking 1-2, 3, 7, 10, 24-5, 43, 48, 53-4, 59, 61-3, 64n, 65, 70, 81, 83, 120, 128, 138, 187n, 192, 199-200
Cromwell, Oliver 113

D

Delphi ix, 16, 21
Democracy 6n, 7, 10, 12, 31, 77, 110n, 111, 111n, 136, 136n, 137n
Deontology vii, 41, 128, 129n, 135-6, 136n, 139, 143-158, 159n, 160, 169
Descartes 4, 100n, 103n, 143
Dialectic vii, 13, 28-30, 32, 173, 196, 200, 205
Diderot, Denis 116-7
Diotima 53
Divine Law 75-6, 85, 88
Du Fu 4
Durkheim, Emile 189n

E

Edinburgh 118
Emotivism 122-3, 138-9, 146, 161, 167-70, 184, 186, 188
Empiricism vii, 11n, 40, 54, 83, 97, 99, 104, 116, 118-22, 129, 143-5, 167-70, 186
Enlightenment 115-8, 129, 161, 178, 179n, 185
Epictetus 59-60, 60n
Epicurus/Epicureanism 55-7, 60, 129
Eros vi, 44, 180, 201-2
Existentialism vii, 174-8, 185, 188

F

Fact/value distinction (see also naturalistic fallacy) 44n, 123-5, 138
Farrer, Austin 81n
Finnis, John 182, 182n
Foot, Philippa 170-1, 171n
Foucault, Michel 180-1, 181n
Francis, St. 127
Free will xi, 5, 47-8, 69-70, 81, 100-5, 136-7, 177
Friendship vi, 1, 42-3, 57, 134, 156, 158, 201, 205
Fry, Elizabeth 203

G

Galileo 40, 98
Gewirth, Alan 182, 182n
Good will 146-50, 152, 191
Grace 69-70, 117, 201
Great Chain of Being 43-6, 104, 175
Grotius, Hugo 86, 86n

H

Hampshire, Stuart 196n
Happiness vii, xii, 19, 41-2, 52, 57, 128-138, 141, 146, 148, 156, 159n, 163-5, 176, 191n
Hare, Richard 136, 182, 182n
Hart, H.L.A. 86, 155, 196-9
Hartshorne, Charles 85n
Hegel, G.W.F. 143, 171, 173
Heraclitus 56
Hick, John 189n
Hinduism 64, 66, 148, 200
Hobbes, Thomas 55, 96-114, 115-6, 119, 120, 133, 143-4, 155, 171, 198

Homer 4, 12, 35, 163, 163n
Homosexuality vii-viii, 14n
Hood, F.C. 109n
Hosea 200, 200n
Human rights 60, 89n, 95, 126, 159, 182, 186, 190-1
Humanae Vitae 92, 92n
Hume, David x, xii, 44n, 115-127, 129, 133, 137-8, 143-6, 160, 167, 176, 185, 192
Huxley, Aldous 189n

I

Idealism viii, 26-7, 36, 40, 56, 61
Immortality 43, 58, 61-2
Ineffability viii, 100
Irony viii, 17, 17n, 75, 179
Isaiah 7
Islam 5, 28, 62, 64, 71, 71n, 85, 88, 117n, 204

J

James, William 196
Jeremiah 7
Jerusalem 65
Jesus 30, 30n, 66, 66n, 69, 71-2, 80n, 117n, 148, 200-2
Jews/Judaism vi, 28, 55, 62, 66-9, 80, 85-6, 105, 117n, 206
Just war 71-8

K

Kafka, Franz 182, 182n
Kant, Immanuel 139, 143-58, 165, 179, 188, 191, 203
Kelsen, H. 172n
Kierkegaard, Soren 175, 175n
Koestler, Arthur 64n

L

Lamont, Corliss ix
Langford, M.J. 152n, 193n
Leibniz 5, 143
Lenin 65
Lyotard, Jean-Francois 179-80, 179n, 180n
Levellers 190
Lincoln, Abraham 136n
Locke, John 111n, 116, 116n, 143
Love (see also agape, eros, philia) vi, 44, 59, 69-70, 76, 120, 146-8, 180, 189, 200-07
Luther, Martin xi, 116
Lying 6, 128-9, 150-3, 151n, 157-8

M

MacIntyre, Alasdair 160-3
Marcuse, Herbert 174, 174n
Marks, Joel 182, 182n
Marx/Marxism vii, 65, 91, 95, 160, 171-4, 176, 178
Materialism 56, 60-1, 98-105, 109, 171-2
McCarthyism 14
Mecca 65
Metaethics 8-10, 157, 160, 167, 188
Metaphor vi, viii-ix, 3-4, 58, 62n, 145, 189n
Metaphysics ix, 5, 8n, 36, 36n, 40, 44, 52, 56-7, 60-1, 80, 99, 103n, 136, 161, 185-7
Micah 206
Miki, Nakayama 53
Mill, James 133, 136n
Mill, J.S. xii, 102-4, 128-42, 143, 154, 159n, 163-4, 191, 191n
Miracles 82n
Monism ix, 58-9

Montesquieu 111n
Moore, G.E. 167, 167n, 170
Moral realism 170-1, 186, 188, 204, 204n
Mozi 5, 72
Murdoch, Iris 201, 201n
Myth ix, 29-30, 32, 49n, 68, 105, 176

N

Nagel, Thomas 103n
Napoleon 124
Natural justice/natural law 46n, 50-1, 71n, 83, 85-9, 93-5, 112, 120, 155, 161-2, 172n, 182, 182n, 197
Naturalistic fallacy (see also fact/value distinction) 4, 170-1
Neoplatonism 43, 60-3, 84, 89, 93
Newton, Isaac 117
Nietzsche, Friedrich 163, 181
Nihilism 181, 185, 192, 194
Nomological impossibility 84, 84n
Norman, Robert xii
Nous 43, 60
Nussbaum, Martha 201, 201n, 202, 202n

O

Omnipotence 71, 81, 83-5
Omniscience 71, 83-5
Ontology ix, 26
Origen 55, 67-9, 69n, 73
Orthodox tradition x, 49n, 79-80, 80n, 90, 173

P

Paine, Thomas 190
Pantheism x, 60n

Parable x, 30, 49n, 68, 119, 201
Parfit, Derek 165
Passion/emotion x, 30, 49, 58, 61, 115, 118-22, 126, 133, 149, 189, 192, 198
Paul, St. 59, 69n, 85, 90
Pelagius 70
Phenomenology x, 105
Philia vi, 1, 42, 201
Philo 66
Philosophical Radicals 132, 132n
Pius XII 77
Plato vi, vii, ix, 2-4, 14n, 15, 18, 21, 25-38, 39-40, 42-4, 45n, 48-9, 51, 53, 56-7, 60-1, 62n, 69, 91, 93, 96-7, 110, 119-20, 122, 144-5, 148-9, 161, 173, 175n, 176, 180, 201-2, 202n, 204n
Plotinus 60, 62, 205
Postmodernism 178-81, 191
Practical ethics 8-9, 54, 63, 136, 157, 159, 162, 167, 188, 205
Predestination xi, 70, 102n
Prescriptivism 181, 182n
Pringle-Pattison, A. Seth 132n
Projectivism 182
Puritanism 30n, 45n, 78
Pythagoras 11n

Q
Quakers/Quakerism 53, 92, 190n, 203

R
Rawls, John 165-7
Reason/rationality 2, 29-30, 45, 49, 58, 63, 93, 105, 115-9, 122, 143-4, 153, 161, 163, 165-7, 182, 186, 191-3, 199-200, 206
Reductionism xi, 100, 102n, 103n, 105, 135n

Index

Religion xi, xii, 2n, 8, 14-5, 27, 30n, 37, 43-5, , 53-5, 58, 63-8, 69, 71-2, 75, 77, 80-1, 85-6, 89-92, 99-100, 109-10, 115-6, 127, 147-8, 175n, 186, 188-90,190n, 198
Rhetoric xi, 13-14, 187, 190

S

Shankara 66
Sartre, Jean-Paul 175-8
Science 11, 11n, 13, 17, 19, 27, 40, 64n, 83, 85, 97-9, 115-8, 129, 135, 139, 143-4, 178, 186
Searle, John 103n
Secularism xi-xii, 37-8, 43, 64, 64n, 71, 71n, 77, 86, 86n, 95, 102, 103n, 134, 161, 172n, 185-6, 190, 203
Shakespeare 4
Sikhism 53
Sin/original sin x, 48n, 70, 90-1, 95, 116, 172n, 173
Singer, Peter 163-5
Smith, Adam 118
Socrates 1-2, 5, 11, 12-24, 25-6, 28, 29, 36-7, 39, 45, 51-2, 53, 57, 67, 134, 161, 175-6, 185, 187, 204
Sophists 13, 30, 51, 56, 101, 162, 185
Southey, Robert, viii
Speciesism 164
Spinoza, Baruch 143, 205n
Stalin 91
State of nature 105-6, 109, 155
Stevenson, Charles 168, 168n, 169, 184-5
Stoicism 43, 55-6, 57-61, 76, 89, 93, 98, 171
Suicide 141-2, 152-3, 157-8
Sympathy 120-2, 133, 146, 167, 198

T

Tenrikyo 53
Thales, 19
Theism xii, 59, 63
Thucydides 117
Tocqueville, Alexis de 137n
Toleration/intolerance 14, 18, 90-1, 91n, 110, 190
Tyranny of the majority 136-7

U

Upanishads 7, 64-5
Urmson, J.O. 168n
Utility/Utilitarianism vi-vii, xii, 9, 41, 42n, 52, 120-2, 128-42, 153-4, 158, 159n, 160, 163-6, 169, 188, 191, 191n, 203

V

Vanstone, W.H. 204n
Vegetarianism 164-5
Vico, Giambattista 11n
Virtue, vi, 19, 30, 30n, 37, 39-54, 57-8, 61, 81-2, 148-9, 153, 160-3, 169, 171, 175, 185, 187, 203, 205
Vitoria, Francisco 74-6, 194
Voltaire 117
Voluntarism 68n
Voluntary/involuntary action (see also free will) 47, 49-50, 52-3, 91, 101, 112

W

Wilde, Lillian 202n
Williams, Bernard 6n
Whitehead, A.N. 25
Wittgenstein, Ludwig 3, 26, 65, 169-70

Wollstonecraft, Mary 191
Woolman, John 190, 190n

X
Xenophon 15

Z
Zeno of Citium 57
Zhu Xi 66
Zoroaster/Zarathustra 7